SUCCESS REBEL

ADVANCE PRAISE

"The timeliness of *Success Rebel* is perfection. It is time for us to wake up and realize the gifts in all of us and to be unapologetic about them, while also being powerful. Ali teaches us how, in her newest book—and in her true way—it gets you headed toward that power immediately."

Kate Taylor—Stylist

"What if you could understand how to have the best partnership of your life—a partnership with the Divine? What if you could access your own unique Divine Soulfire, a powerful force that will lead you to accomplish your mission here on earth in a way that is beyond your wildest dreams?

You can!

Ali's amazing book, *Success Rebel: How To Be Sought After And Successful Without Selling Your Soul*, shows you exactly how.

This book takes you to the seat of your greatest power and creativity and activates your blueprint for deep fulfillment and success! Definitely get your copy and get started now!"

Dr. Diana Kirschner—International bestselling author of "Love in 90 Days"

"This book changes the game. And Ali changes the way you approach success. She makes it seem more attainable than ever. And isn't that refreshing?"

Sasha Safdiah—Founder@faceunited

"The message of this book is an "action" plan to deliberately create all aspects of your life with REAL and PRACTICAL implementable tools—to become the Master within you! Kick butt steps to success! You are "shown" through the brilliance of the language in this book how resolving the emotional issues in your tissues from your "sometimes secretive or sometimes know" inside world—to consciously change your outside world—through artfully crafted solutions. You eliminate the known or unknown blocks that have held you hostage or continue to hold you back from your success in all aspects of your life! This is YOUR SUCCESS BOOK!"

Sherry Anshara—Founder of
The Anshara Method

"I've known Ali for years, and one thing that has always impressed me about her is how she is able to create multiple successful businesses on HER TERMS. She is always unapologetically herself and her businesses reflects that, even when it means bucking conventional wisdom or all the well-meaning "you need to do like this" advice. What I love about *Success Rebel* is how she captured the essence of her secrets to success in this book, and she did it in a way to make it easy to follow and implement. I highly recommend this book."

Michele PW, Bestselling, Award-Winning
Author

SUCCESS REBEL

How To Be Sought After and Successful Without Selling Your Soul

Ali Craig

GIRL WITH DRIVE PRESS

Girl With Drive Press
9221 E Baseline Rd Ste A109-600
Mesa, AZ
85209
www.girlwithdrivepress.com
(347)215.4091

Ordering Information:

Quantity sales. Special discounts are available on
quantity purchases by corporations, associations,
and others. For details, contact the publisher at the
address above. Orders by U.S. trade bookstores and
wholesalers.

Printed in the United States of America
PRINT: ISBN: 978-1-7322841-1-1
DIGITAL: Also Available
The main category of the book—Interpersonal
Relationships
First Edition
14 13 12 11 10 / 10 9 8 7 6 5 4 3 2 1

TRADEMARK DISCLAIMER:

Hey, Beaut!

In this book you will see me address a lot of businesses and use a lot of terms. Many of these businesses are mine each held under distinct LLC's. Also, you will see a few trademark terms along the way. Such as:

> 7 Figure Signals™
> EmpiHER®
> Entreventure®
> Fix My Brand With Ali Craig®
> Intelligent Influence™
> NERI®
> Neuro Human Branding®
> Notoriety™
> Soulfire®
> Success Rebel™

These trademarks are held by one of my various LLC entities. Please go to each company's website for all the legal 411 as well as the latest skinny.

Love + Gratitude,

Ali

Table of Contents

Introduction   xv

What You Need To Know   1

Are You A Success Rebel   7

#1 Reason Why You Fail To Succeed   11

How The Cult Of The Others Is Killing
  Your Success   21

Why We All Secretly Want To Be Notorious   29

Don't Let Your Soulfire Die Inside Of You   37

Why Being The Best Matters   43

Why Your Desire To Be Known Matters
(And Is A Good Thing)   49

What Are You Really Capable Of   55

The "What Ifs" Or A Winning Life   63

Power Of Possibilities   69

The Circus Of Life   77

The True Heart Of The Matter   89

Why You Must First Be Happy
  To Be Successful   97

Being Good At Sex Makes You Good
  At Being Successful   105

The Struggle For Success Myth   111

Why Life And Love Don't Go Hand In Hand   119

Get Your Heart On Straight First   125

The Ultimate Hurt   143

The Ultimate Test You Must Pass To Live A
Successful Life   149

Your Dreams Have It   159

Why Change Is Overrated   169

Why You Must Be Able To Define Success
On Your Own Terms   181

How To Go From Struggle To Flow
In Every Aspect Of Your Life   187

Why "The Line In The Sand Of Soon"
Lifestyle Is Killing Your Success
And The Dreams Of Others   195

The Plan For Your Life   205

Pause, Plan and Pivot   213

Why You Should Be Like Einstein   219

How To Win At Anything   227

Sex, Love, and Disruption   233

Instant Success Through Energetic Income   245

Put Your Mind On Your Motive and
Your Motive On Your Mind   255

Words, Work, Worth, And Wealth   261

Why Nice "Guys" Don't Matter   271

Why Everyone Must Have "I.T."   279

Why Being Failure Obsessed Creates More
Failure   287

How To Create Relationships That Work   293

How To Own Any Room Without
  Ever Saying A Word   301

Will The Real You Please Stand Up?   309

Energy. Instinct. Environment.   317

How Winning Mario Brothers Makes You
  A Winner In Life   325

Influence. Intention. Inspection.   331

The Lie That Solo Equals Success   335

Never Back Down   339

Appendix   341

About the Author   348

Acknowledgements   351

Dedication   353

INTRODUCTION

My favorite game growing up was the *Game of Life*. It made life seem interesting, but safe. It also made success seem attainable no matter what life path came my way.

Clearly, success is something with which I have always been obsessed. I've learned you don't try to write your first book at age eight because you thought your friends would think you were cool. You do it because you want your life to matter, to make a difference, and if a little bit of fame, fortune, and financial success comes your way too—you aren't going to say "no" to it.

Like many Gen X-ers. The idea and pursuit of success is something we all crave. Throughout the last twenty years, I have helped countless clients, magazine readers, national TV viewers, and event attendees get one step closer to have the version of success they see in their dreams.

For many though, success doesn't come because people pursue a dream or vision that is destined to fail. Because no, not everyone is cut out to do everything. And the way I am designed to succeed isn't the way you are. I hate to break it to you—all of those "do as I did" or "follow my method" approaches for the most part get the creator rich and you poor.

This book, *Success Rebel: How To Be Sought After and Successful Without Selling Your Soul* dives into all of this. It goes way beyond just being a book. We delve into the what, how and why some people succeed, and others simply struggle. I am going to share with you personal stories, hacks, and the systems that I created over the years to help my clients and myself overcome what was holding us back in life, business, and brands when it comes to living the success of our dreams.

Most importantly it is my firm belief and declaration that the desires of your heart are possible and that you are no accident. This book has graced your path because it is time for you to step out of the societally induced amnesia in which you have been living—and step into your dreams, destiny, and the life of influence, grace, and notoriety you have always desired.

Chapter 1

WHAT YOU NEED TO KNOW

I'll be honest with you. This isn't the book I set out to write. The idea of being a Success Rebel™ is one that has percolated in my heart and mind, and throughout my work for years. I honestly thought this book was going to be a book based on owning your personal brand. On some levels it is, but as you will discover, it goes so much further.

Let's be real, most people won't ever feel qualified to claim, own, or say, that "I have done IT," "made IT," and "I have nothing left to achieve." I know I felt that way for a long time because in my heart of hearts there was always more to achieve, do, and become. Thus, I set out to write and this was the book that appeared. And when the Divine guides the words, you write them down—if you are smart.

These pages blend all of my efforts over the last twenty plus years of working with the minds, hearts, and emotions of hundreds of thousands of people from around the world. The truth about branding isn't what most people think.

Branding isn't what you do to livestock— at least not this kind of branding. And yes, that bad pun is for the guys out there.

Branding is all about the relationship with self and others, with the common first point of connection being a product, service, or company.

I'm going to bet that is not a definition or framework you have ever truly thought about branding. I know this because that isn't how The OTHERS talk about or teach branding. But trust me, as an international NEURO HUMAN BRANDING and INTELLIGENT INFLUENCE consultant for over twenty years—I know a lot about brands, business, and success both in life and work.

I can honestly tell you that this book is proof of the principles it puts forth. I have been the mere hands and feet to this project while the source of the wisdom comes from something far greater than me— something that frames my life's work in a way in which I was even shocked.

But before you jump on into the transformational, action focused message you are about to experience, you first need the five ground rules on what to expect and not expect from this book.

DON'T SAY I DIDN'T WARN YOU!

1. GET READY TO BUCK THE SYSTEM.

This book is a no holds barred, unapologetic, not politically correct book. If you enjoy such beliefs as "get rich quick with no consistent work," "believe it and it will magically be," or that because you are unique you are entitled to anything you want with no effort. Please! Put this book down and go watch Netflix.

Success Rebel: How To Be Sought After and Successful Without Selling Your Soul goes against most social norms, stories, and the politically correct agenda of today. We believe success is possible and that the tide of your success can change at a moment's notice because you have consistently been the hands and feet of your Divinely planted dreams.

2. LOVE INSPIRATION, IDEAS, AND ACTION.

This book will inspire you to go beyond your norm and reach for the dreams of greatness that lie within you. But if you aren't going to take action, don't waste your time. Inspiration is great, but it is like masturbation. It gets you off, but that's it.

Self-gratification is not what you are here for if you are seriously looking for true, epic levels of success.

AT ITS CORE, EPIC, WORLD CHANGING, AND
LIFE-CHANGING SUCCESS IS ALWAYS BECAUSE
YOU ARE OF SERVICE TO OTHERS NOT
YOURSELF.

So, if you are only looking for the solo feelings—f*ck
off would you.

3. SUCCESS AND SPIRITUALITY GO HAND IN HAND.

I one hundred percent believe that success and
spirituality go hand in hand. As a Christian woman,
I talk about God with words such as Jesus, the
Divine, Creator and Providence. I use such terms
interchangeably to refer to the One who created us
and all of this around us—seen and unseen.

If this language isn't in alignment with your beliefs
simply flip out the word for the noun that works for
you. And if you can't wrap your head around that a
Big Bang didn't create us, "Bye, Feltcha."

Then seriously, put this book down and walk away.
It won't be for you.

Now you also may be thinking, "Yes! A Christian
sister in the business space who doesn't look like
they came from 'Little House On The Prairie.'
Preach it!" Please know that yes, I am a Bible
believing Christian woman who knows that my life is

nothing without the Creator. But know that I believe in a relationship not a religion.

Social stories aren't off limits, nor is the misinformation that many churches have used over the decades to distort the word of God and limit the scope of our lives.

With that said, I like you, am not perfect and nor do I claim to be. Being a Christian doesn't mean you are perfect. It means that I know in the end the greatest aspects of what I bring aren't from me. I am not claiming to teach you the Bible and nor do I want to convert you. This is just me.

4. LEAVE YOUR HANG UPS AT THE FRONT COVER.

I have been a luxury neuro human brander for over twenty years. I always tell my branding clients that branding is a deeply personal experience. Success is no exception.

This book will trigger you, shock you, make you cry, piss you off, have your internal lightbulb go off more times than you can count, and inspire you to action. If that doesn't sound like scary fun, then don't read this book. If you aren't willing to change, grow, and evolve—go pick up some feel-good fluff instead.

5. LEARN. DO. BELIEVE. BECOME. CONNECT.

This is not your typical book. I am not your typical author. I am all about information and action. These chapters aren't long and fluffy. They aren't filled with 97% stories to help inspire you to change, but nothing to tell you how to at least start.

This book is filled with truth, what works, and what it really takes to have what you say you want. At the beginning of each chapter I set the intention for the transformational space I hold for you with words to engage you.

At the end of each chapter, there are quick ways to take action with what you just learned. Based on where you are at in your SUCCESS REBEL journey, you can choose the action that best suits you. The LEARN, DO, BELIEVE, BECOME. CONNECT sections are all designed to tap into the fundamental cores of what makes you "you" while creating the maximum amount of change and growth possible at one time.

OK, that's what to expect from *Success Rebel: How To Be Sought After and Successful Without Selling Your Soul.*

Are you ready for the rebellion to begin?

Chapter 2

ARE YOU A SUCCESS REBEL

MAY YOUR HEART AND MIND BEGIN TO BREAK FREE OF THE SOCIAL TIES THAT STRANGLE YOUR DIVINELY IMPLANTED SUCCESS.

We are a society obsessed with success. Personal success, professional success, financial success, physical success, mental success—being the best in all aspects of your life is the American way. We are taught to excel, win, conquer, grow, achieve, build, do, lead. Success is expected to prove your value, to be happy, to be loved, liked, and everything in between.

But really is it?

Though we live in a society that talks about and praises epic, monumental levels of success, achievement on such levels isn't something the majority of people experience in any area of their lives. We talk about it. We claim to model it through modern day social stories like movies and television shows about what it should look like, feel like, and what it means to have it.

A quick Google search and you can find a minimum of 3,730,000,000 resource filled results on how to be successful in an area of your life. From getting rich quick schemes to the wisdom of Napoleon Hill and King Solomon. In spite of all this information, there clearly are very few results.

Most people live a life of struggle, unknown, and survival. The idea of thriving and having influence, let alone living a life of NEW NOTORIETY, is a fairy tale dream. And let's face it, having Prince Charming ride up with a glass slipper in hand has a greater potential for happening than achieving the levels of success you dream of.

Why is that? The answer is simple.

THE ACT OF BEING SUCCESSFUL IS PRAISED, BUT THE ACTS THAT GET YOU THERE GO AGAINST THE SOCIAL PROGRAMMING OF WHAT IS RIGHT, PROPER, GOOD, AND HOLY.

Let's get real. Though the personal and professional development industries combined currently generate well over $30 billion dollars in revenue annually, most of us understand the detailed logistics of a mission to the moon just as much as we do on how to be successful.

Though society says they want you to be a great success—control, culture, and carrying social expectations are more important. To get to such levels of success, you must go against the norm. You must choose to reprogram your mind, heart, expectations, and desired outcomes. You must choose to be a rebel against a lifetime of programming to reconnect to your Source of success—in your unique way.

So, what do you choose?

LEARN

The status quo won't get you the success your heart dreams of.

Do.
Begin to question the motives behind the messages you are receiving.

BELIEVE.
Know without a shadow of a doubt that your raw, unbiased dreams can be your reality.

BECOME.
Evaluate what you say you want and who you say you want to be. Begin to consciously choose how, when, and where you show up.

CONNECT.
Going against the social norms is designed to be a very lonely and isolating road, but it doesn't have to be. Use media outlets, social media, and groups to your advantage. Embrace situations that test your skills to uncover and observe the social biases we all have. And when you are looking for a "safe space" to connect with likeminded SUCCESS REBELS, we provide an entire list of resources listed in the back of this book—and at http://SuccessRebelBook.com.

Chapter 3

#1 REASON WHY YOU FAIL TO SUCCEED

MAY YOU RECOGNIZE ON A CELLULAR CHANGING LEVEL THAT YOU ARE DESIGNED TO HAVE A GREATER IMPACT AND INFLUENCE THAN YOUR CURRENT LIFE REFLECTS.

If desire was enough to create a successful life, we would all have one. Success is far deeper than the physicalities of life. True success comes down to our souls. The reason why we are here on this planet today.

MANY PEOPLE FAIL TO PAUSE AND RECOGNIZE THE SCOPE OF WHO AND WHAT THEY REALLY ARE AND ARE REALLY CAPABLE OF.

But if we would recognize the true power we innately have, then we would realize that the success in our heart isn't too far away.

When I started in this field, what most people know now as branding, back in the late '90s was the traditional approach for consumer interactions— what I call the "Tag You're It" model. This is where the company would say whatever they wanted to the consumer and then essentially run away from the conversation. This left the consumer wondering what to do or perusing the company for more information. But because the consumer pursued the company these marketing campaigns were considered quite memorable.

Who among us doesn't remember the Sears' Toy Book every Christmas season? Or that Toys Я Us had really exotic and expensive toys. Or that little ol' lady who only found the beef at Wendy's.

Traditional marketing was about sharing their message, not creating a conversation.

Though smart to create desirability, psychological buy in, and all the while playing to the social story of the ego, this approach fails to serve any audience on a fundamental level. The human one.

Honestly, this approach never made sense to me because it never recognized that in the end, both the companies and their consumers are people. And in that single fact alone, there is great power, commonality, connection, and influence.

What do old marketing campaigns have to do with success? Marketing and branding are all about the relationship between you and the business. Success is all about the relationship between you and your dreams. Yes, success isn't something you check off your "to do" list or something you simply become.

SUCCESS IS A RELATIONSHIP.

As with any relationship, the more successful ones have thoughtfulness, intentionality, and a desire for both to win. Good relationships take into consideration how someone will best receive the message that needs to be shared and then adjusts their approach, tone, timing, energy, and words accordingly. It is from this human belief the branding method known as, NEURO HUMAN BRANDING, was born. The truth is though that the three core areas of NEURO HUMAN BRANDING: BIOLOGY, SUBCONSCIOUS MIND, and SOCIAL STORIES affect our relationships with others and our ability to succeed.

If we look at success as the relationship it truly is, most of us don't understand how we are supposed to relate to it. We go through life interacting with success like the brides and grooms do on the reality TV show, *Love At First Sight*. The people whom the participants are about to marry are supposed to be the loves of their lives, but they have no known common points of connection. They don't know what makes the other happy, sad, fearful, excited—what really makes them tick. Time eventually works the situation out on the TV show; unfortunately, that isn't the case with success.

BECAUSE WE DON'T KNOW HOW TO RELATE TO SUCCESS WE SIMPLY DON'T.

We aren't married to it and we can walk away from the relationship and return back to it as many times as we want. Creating confusion, dysfunctional relationships, and playing into the social stories that success is an enigma. Simply put, we aren't able to have a happy and productive relationship with success.

The following includes a few truths about success and you.

BIOLOGY: SUCCESS IS IN YOUR DNA.

Yes, you truly were designed to live a life of your dreams. Yes, success is truly in your DNA.

As our understanding about genes has evolved over the last twenty years, numerous studies from around the world have come out, noting the level of success reached is based off of our DNA. And though true, it is interesting to note that as with all of our genes, both expression and repression can occur.

Gene expression and repression, also known as gene regulation, can occur for many reasons. Currently the overall scientific belief is that environment, and overall life cycles are the biggest contributing factors.

Yet, as we begin to understand the true power of the mind, scientists are beginning to realize that our mindset can also play just as vital a role in our gene regulation. Which in turn means that our minds can either activate our DNA for success or repress the potential that lies within.

SUBCONSCIOUS MIND: YOUR ROAD MARKER TO SUCCESS.

All of those secret desires for who you want to be, what you want to achieve, and become are planted deep inside of you because they are your unique road markers to guide you through life.

Our subconscious mind controls 95% of our life and our understanding of it. It remembers everything; it records everything from what it sees, to what it feels, including the secret desires of our heart—our dreams even—from a very young age. And because the subconscious mind forgets nothing, throughout our lives, these Divine dreams will re-emerge.

When this happens many of us ignore the re-emerging dream. We wait for them to go away or convert them into a practical goal that makes more logical sense and is in alignment with the modern-day social stories of success. The good news? No matter what you do or don't do—the core heart of your passions, the fantasies that used to take your mind over as a young kid, those tasks that you were inexplicably good at—all of that is still inside of you.

Now modern-day social stories and THE OTHERS would like for you to believe that your subconscious mind is simply a bad fairytale.

IT IS YOUR RESPONSIBILITY TO USE YOUR BIOLOGY AND THE POWER THAT LIES WITHIN YOU TO YOUR ADVANTAGE.

Because no one else has the unique dreams, visions, and ideas that you do.

That is what makes you unique. And it is our responsibility to guard these dreams, hold them tight, and make them happen. It is also our responsibility to unearth the truth of our dreams from our subconscious mind and not allow the outward pressures of The OTHERS to influence how we take action.

SOCIAL STORIES: REBEL WITH A CLUE.

To truly be successful you must go against a lot of norms. In many forms—familial, parental, regional, religious, or societal expectations—and then the larger social stories of what a person like you, where you are from, and with your background, can or cannot be capable of. Stories like:

- Sticking it to "the man."

- Believing girls are always so bad with money.

- Succeeding outside of your hometown.

- Making sure that women marry wealthy men.

- Questioning who and what makes a "real" man.

And then we have all of those "Who would want you if" stories. Who would want you if:

- You don't want that classic 2.5 kids, a dog, and home in the suburb's lifestyle?

- You make more money than your partner?

- Don't have a "stable" job?

- You lose money?

- You fail?

It is stories like these that have been told to you and implanted in you before you were even born. Just because these stories have been ingrained into your psyche doesn't mean that they won't go away. But you have to be willing to rebel against all you have ever known, been taught, or have been told about who you are if you truly want to succeed and live a life of NEW NOTORIETY.

Look at the word "rebel" for a moment. What comes to the internal movie screen of your mind when you say the word "rebel?" What have you been taught about rebels?

Here is what most people think of.

- Rebels aren't smart. They don't think.

- Rebels act carelessly and die young.

- Rebels never succeed; they cause problems and hurt the ones they love.

- Rebels are selfish, mean, and are bullies on many levels.

- Rebels do drugs, create drama, and take no responsibility for their actions.

- Rebels are moody, depressed, and never have love in their lives.

- Rebels are the silent "bad boy" types.

With those general social stories about rebels playing in your heads and bodies on a nonstop loop, why would you want to rebel even if the payoff was living your dreams, being a success, and living a life of influence, grace, and notoriety?

Simply put you wouldn't.

And clearly as a society at large we don't. We don't want to get kicked out of our tribe. We don't want to be troublemakers. We don't want to cause pain for others. We don't want to hurt others. We don't want to be depressed, alone, and unloved.

The fundamental cores of human beings are all the same. We want to:

(1) Give and receive unconditional love —aka love,

(2) Know we have people we can rely on—aka certainty,

(3) Have some fun—aka variety,

(4) Grow and evolve—aka growth,

(5) Give back to others—aka contribution.

(6) Matter to the people around us—aka significance.

That is Human Needs Psychology in a nutshell.

No matter who you are, where you were born, when you were born, or what has happened to you in your life, these six needs you have simply because you are human.

We are taught that if we engage in any form of rebellion that everyone and everything that meets our human needs will go away. So why would we try for the hope and the prayer of success? We wouldn't and "smart" people don't.

LEARN.

No matter what people say, you are fully capable of being, living, and evolving into the person you have always dreamed of. Check out my BREAK FREE HACK that helps you overcome the social stories that are holding you back. Grab your digital copy for free at http://SuccessRebelBook.com.

DO.

Take time from your busy schedule and daydream. Imagine yourself achieving your dreams and living the life of NEW NOTORIETY you have always desired.

BELIEVE.

Your thoughts are more powerful than you have ever imagined. Recognize this power and then use it wisely.

BECOME.

Take an audit of everything and everyone to whom you expose yourself every day. From the music you listen to—to the small talk on the elevator, or the TV show you fall asleep to each night—become consciously aware of the stories, tones, and energies these people and things produce.

CONNECT.

Reconnect with your childhood dreams. Think back to your earliest memories of what made you happy and ask yourself, "why?" Then find new ways to live that "why" today.

Chapter 4

HOW THE CULT OF THE OTHERS IS KILLING YOUR SUCCESS

MAY YOU BREAK FREE OF THE MENTAL STRONGHOLDS THAT ARE UNKNOWINGLY SABOTAGING THE DESIRES OF YOUR HEART AND YOUR SUCCESS.

You see, as long as humanity has been around we have had ITS and The OTHERS. The ITS are what brings us joy, makes the world better, creates beauty, shows love, and transcends the physicality of one's soul. I call this your SOULFIRE because they light up your soul in a way that nothing else does for you—or does for anyone else.

These "ITS" truly are the Divine purpose for why we are here. And for many of us they create a feeling of fire inside of our hearts—aka SOULFIRE. Your SOULFIRE may not sound sexy, glamorous, or the road to your ultimate success, but it fuels you, excites you, and is effortless for you to birth.

The OTHERS on the other hand seem right. Logically, what they preach seems like a nice thing to do, sounds smart, gives us lots to do, and feels empowering in the beginning. But becomes an unbearable weight soon enough. The OTHERS teach you to stop thinking and start doing.

That "doing' is the way to success, love, life, happiness, acceptance, and fulfillment. Doing is the way in which your personal, emotional, mental, spiritual, and physical needs are met. Doing is the only way to secure your importance, status, and value in this life.

And that doing is all there is in this life.

The OTHERS don't want you to see, think, or know about the future. Their mindset is that if you can think about a future be it three hours from now, three years from now, three decades from now, or an eternity from now—you clearly aren't doing enough. If you aren't doing enough what is your current value now?

Nothing and nobody.

BUT WHAT IF I SAID THAT THE OTHERS, THEIR PRESSURE, THEIR BURDENS, THEIR RULES WERE

ALL AN ILLUSION TO STOP YOU FROM BEING, DOING, AND LIVING YOUR DIVINE PURPOSE?

What if I told you that the wants, desires, dreams, and "ITS" are Divinely placed in you just like jewels in a crown —hand selected, perfectly chosen, with thoughtfulness, intention, and love?

What if I told you that the stories that run through your head are not?

- "Who are you?,"
- "Success, notoriety are bad,"
- "You are going to get hurt,"
- "People will reject you,"
- "You will have no one and nothing."

Each is a veiled threat to control you, weaken you, and keep you under mental, emotional, and physical control just like a cult.

What if I told you it is possible to break free? That it is easier than you think. That living a life of NEW NOTORIETY is a really good thing—when you live it on your terms and with your SOULFIRE firmly at the core?

What if I told you that this life of success and NEW NOTORIETY, which you divinely and desperately seek, is one thought away? One switch of the mind is all it takes to go from the repression of The OTHERS to stepping into your unique IT. Your SOULFIRE.

It's true.

It is all possible.

**EVERYTHING YOU NEED YOU ALREADY HAVE.
YOU SIMPLY HAVE TO MAKE THE MENTAL
SWITCH TO SEE THE GIFTS THAT SURROUND
YOU.**

LEARN.

The stories and expectations that have been indoctrinated into you since birth is social inoculation of mass mindset mentality.

DO.

Question the whens, wheres, and whys, that define your daily life.

BELIEVE.

Breaking from a cult mindset starts with a crack. You don't need to know everything—to know you know enough.

BECOME.

Choose to lose the pressure, unfulfillment, mental and emotional berating meant by The OTHERS and step into the lighthearted, joy filled, excitement that is meant to be your success-filled life. Welcome to your life of NEW NOTORIETY.

CONNECT.

A successful life is about choice and connections. Begin to make conscious choices about who, when, and why you are building these relationships. If Harry and Meghan can break free, so can you.

1

OWN, IDENTIFY, AND TAKE ACTION ON YOUR POTENTIAL, POSSIBILITIES, PURPOSE, AND POWER

Chapter 5

WHY WE ALL SECRETLY WANT TO BE NOTORIOUS

MAY WE PURSUE UNBIASEDLY WHAT SPARKS OUR SOULS.

If you were being really honest—you know, the type of honesty you rarely share with the deepest parts of yourself—somewhere deep inside, you know you want to be notorious.

Yes, notorious. You want to be the best, the known, the infamous, the world changing, badass of whatever matters to you. Some people want to be notoriously wealthy, popular, industry leaders, or business titans. While others want to be notoriously known for being an outstanding dad, best wife, the ultimate aunt, friend, or volunteer.

No matter what you want to be notorious for, you desire notoriety because it means you are the ultimate success at whatever it is you've been striving for.

But let's be honest, the word notorious makes you feel a bit like a bad boy, or girl, right? The word, notorious, brings out the swagger, the unapologetic, and bold confidence. And if you are a child of the '80s and '90s like me, you can't help but think of Notorious BIG and that whole East Coast/ West Coast rivalry.

The more highly evolved lot would say that such a desire to be notorious was rooted from our ego. Therefore, because the ego isn't highly evolved, we should suppress it at all cost. After all, we are civilized, logical, and intelligent beings. *Raise your pinky finger high as you toast yourself and your ego driven arrogance!*

What sparks our hearts and our egos to have us and our lives matter to the level of notoriety is something not based on logic. It isn't even conscious. But it is very powerful. This desire for a life of success and notoriety roots from the most primal areas of our being. It comes from where our sub primal nature and our true origin collide. It comes from Providence. It comes from the Divine.

Yes, at the deepest roots of who we are and where we come from is the spark of the Divine. And it is the Divine that wants us to succeed.

And a spark it is—literally. When your Daddy's sperm and Momma's egg connected to form you a spark literally happened. Back in 2016, Northwestern University observed that a spark truly does occur when you are conceived. I firmly believe that the spark that started you, is still inside of you. This spark developed you into a living, breathing, functioning, human being. Therefore, why wouldn't that spark continue the rest of the work your life is meant for?

Why, then, do so many of us hide our truest desires from others and even ourselves? Why do we suppress, ignore, and fail to even acknowledge the desires that are innately planted? What is it in us that stops us from being us?

Nothing.

IT ISN'T US AT ALL.

As kids, we didn't stop ourselves from playing, exploring, having fun, living, laughing, and loving— The OTHERS did. Now these Others show up as friends, loved ones, and well-meaning adults. Though their logical intentions were good. Their subconscious intentions weren't one hundred percent theirs nor were they designed for the betterment of you or them.

You see, having a desire to matter, make a difference, change an industry, transform the world—though noble and on some level socially—is encouraged on a large level. In reality, however, it is greatly discouraged by our most intimate and influential relationships.

Instead of being encouraged on going after the emotional and experiential transformations so many of us intuitively have, especially as kids, our desire for notoriety, success, and achievement are refocused to more "noble" pursuits like being the best in sports and schools.

THE ACT OF BEING SUCCESSFUL IS PRAISED, BUT THE ACTS THAT GET YOU THERE GO AGAINST THE SOCIAL PROGRAMMING OF WHAT IS RIGHT, PROPER, GOOD, AND HOLY.

As we grow and mature our focus is turned even more into the pursuit of money, houses, cars— anything of status. And in turn outward success and old, ego driven notoriety.

YES, WE HAVE BEEN TAUGHT THAT NOTORIETY, OR AS I LIKE TO CALL IT "OLD" NOTORIETY, ARE THE CHAMPAGNE WISHES AND CAVIAR DREAMS LIFESTYLE THAT WE ALL GREW UP SEEING ON THE LIFESTYLE OF THE RICH AND FAMOUS.

That status is everything. From lifestyle to relationships, cars to clothes it is what these things that being, living, doing, and having a life of notoriety and in turn success equates to.

But this old idea of notoriety, the power, success, and status driven life have nothing to do with what you truly want. Such status symbols aren't what lights your heart up and honestly it just doesn't feel right. So, when push comes to shove, the work and effort it takes to create such an inauthentic way of life isn't worth it to you. It isn't worth losing the relationships, love, acceptance, happiness, and joy for some things that don't mean anything to your soul.

The OTHERS know this. They are totally fine with you thinking that the life and lifestyle they have been telling you to seek, want, conquer, get, and keep your entire life isn't what you want. Because they know that by the time you realize this isn't the life you want, many of us have forgotten that the spark that started it all—us, our passion, our life's purpose—ever really existed.

We believe the lies of "who am I." That the idea of living a life of notoriety is nothing you want because you don't want what they are selling. The OTHERS are hoping that you are tired, worn out, confused, and are so mass focused on the social stories of life that you fail to think for yourself and what story you want for your life.

But when you get quiet with yourself and close your eyes, you feel that spark. It may be faint, but it is there. That desire to have a life where what you create in this world transforms it. A transformation on a level that you find it difficult to put your work and life into a social box or even concisely articulate.

Hang tight.

IT IS THAT SPARK THAT YOU MUST NURTURE BECAUSE THAT IS YOUR UNIQUE SPARK OF SUCCESS.

Know that you are not alone.

You are not crazy.

There is a way to take this spark, fan the flame, and build the success driven life of your dreams.

Let me show you how.

LEARN.

The ideas, people, and things that spark your soul is what will spark your success.

DO.

Get clear on what you really want. Write a list of everything you think being successful is. From what you own, to where you live; from what you wear, who you hang out with, etc. The next on the list is to ask yourself, "why?" If you have a logical reason with no heart stirring reaction, it may not be your version of success after all.

BELIEVE.

Never forget that you started from a spark, and the fire still grows, builds, and produces. Your possibilities cease only when you are back on the other side of Heaven.

BECOME.

Step into the Divine energy that is inside of you. Own the fact that you have purpose, value, and a message that people need to hear. Even if you may not be able to articulate it at this moment—it is still inside of you.

CONNECT.

The spark of conception is unseen to most except the Divine. Even as you grow in your mother's womb, only the Creator knows all of your idiosyncrasies and depths. Connect with your heart and Divinity first before you decide to share your spark with others. Head on over to http://successrebelsociety.com to download the audio track of me personally teaching you how to do just that.

Chapter 6

DON'T LET YOUR SOULFIRE DIE INSIDE OF YOU

MAY THE SPARK THAT STARTED YOU TURN INTO A RAGING FIRE THAT INSPIRES YOU.

It may sound like nice pleasantries that we have all heard spouted throughout our lives, "We are here for a purpose." But it is true. You and I are no accident. And because we are no accidents, that creates an awful lot of similarities and common ground to connect on.

Yes, the mainstream media would like for us to believe that as human beings we are radically different. That the areas of commonality are few and far between. That our differences are all that we can see. That we are incapable of relating, understanding, or having relationships with another human being unless we are from the same background, think the same way, look the same or hold the same beliefs as the other person. And without all of this we are fundamentally incapable of being able to connect.

BUT THE TRUTH IS THAT AS A HUMAN BEING WE ARE MORE ALIKE THAN DIFFERENT. LIKE 99.9% ALIKE.

Your genome, basically all of your DNA and genes, is made up of 33 billion base pairs. A 99.9 percent match means that 2.999 billion base pairs are exactly the same for you, me, and the rest of humanity.

One of Albert Einstein's greatest equations, $E = mc^2$, isn't just the foundation to modern physics. It also can be viewed as proof that the spark that created you—that very energy can transform into matter— aka you, your life, your future success. But so, then, can your thoughts, words, and beliefs. It is all energy which means it can transform into matter as well.

Clearly you are no accident.

Now, the title of this chapter is a bit deceiving because of course the spark that started you and the Divine that gave you your SOULFIRE can't die. But the unique partnership that your soul is meant to have on this earth with the Divine surely can.

LIKE WITH ANY RELATIONSHIP, YOU HAVE TO WORK AT IT TO DEVELOP, EVOLVE, AND GROW SOMETHING WORTHWHILE.

Many of us allow this to happen because we think that no other human being can relate—that there will be no other soul on this planet that will understand our heart, message, or mission. That if we put ourselves out there, all of our efforts will fall on deaf ears.

But the truth is we are more alike. We innately connect on biological, spiritual, emotional, and energetic levels. Don't believe me? Well did you know:

HEART.

- The heart is in constant two-way communication with your brain.

- Our emotions change the signals our brain sends and in turn how our heart responds.

- Feeling positive emotions create stronger, more unified, and consistent heart rhythms.

- The heart's electromagnetic field is 100 percent greater in amplitude to the brain's electromagnetic field. This means that people can feel your heart's electromagnetic field.

- The electromagnetic field of the heart is 5,000 times greater than the brain's field.

  *Learn more about the power of the human heart at http://Heartmath.com

CHAKRAS.

- Chakras are energy centers within the body, which help to regulate our organs, immune system, and emotions.

- Chakras communicate energetically—from one person's right side to the other person's left side.

- Chakras align with various Meridian points in the body.

- The Vedas believe Chakras define the seven types of relationships that we can have.

HUMAN NATURE.

- Color psychologically affects us all, no matter when or where you are born.

- We communicate nonverbally over 93% of the time.

- Healthy human relationships decrease cortisol levels.

- We all have the same six core-motives to what makes life fulfilling and happy—aka Human Needs Psychology.

OUR HUMAN NATURE ACTUALLY CONNECTS US MORE THAN IT DIVIDES US.

It is said that many times God keeps us on this side of Heaven because He is giving us every opportunity to fulfill the DIVINE PARTNERSHIP we came here to fulfill. It is true. You are here to make a difference.

LEARN.

No matter what the media tells you, human beings are more alike than we are different.

DO.

Delve deeper to discover how the human body and mind really work.

BELIEVE.

Our words are only one part of the larger message and impression we are making.

BECOME.

A life of influence, success, and notoriety occurs when you master the verbal, nonverbal, and energetic communications that lie within you.

CONNECT.

Once you know intellectually what you are truly capable of, begin to test the theories out on yourself. How do you feel around certain colors? Can you control how far your heart's electromagnetic field goes? Begin to connect with your body to tap into the Divine power that lies within you.

Chapter 7

WHY BEING THE BEST MATTERS

MAY YOUR ACTIONS, PASSIONS, DRIVES, RELATIONSHIPS, AND MOTIVES ALWAYS SET YOUR SOUL ON FIRE.

We all have one.

From the time we come out of the womb, we have an IT. You know IT as a desire, need, or want. I call it your SOULFIRE.

SOULFIRE IS FOR ALL THE MISFITS,
MISUNDERSTOOD, AND MISLABELED WHO SEEK
BRILLIANCE IN THEIR MADNESS, BRING
MEANING TO THEIR PASSIONS, AND DEPTH TO
THE HUMAN EXISTENCE WHO ARE DRIVEN TO BE
CREATORS NOT JUST CREATIVE, WHO ARE LOVE
FOCUSED AND LIFE CENTERED.

Life is not meant to be boring and bland. It is meant to be filled with rich beauty, bold color, tons of laughter, and relationships, which the fairy tales told us were only romantic possibilities. Lighting your passions on fire, fueling your inspiration, and recharging your heart in a fun entertaining way— that's our goal—to discover what life should be.

Our SOULFIRES can sometimes be primal and basic. At other times they are soul stirring reminders, which light us up from the inside—from an unexplainable connection to music, movement, to expressing yourself through some other artistic medium. Other times it is a connection with a sport or act where the world fades away and it is only you in a particular moment.

There is no logical explanation on why these desires, this SOULFIRE, exits. You just have a deep desire to express yourself. And when you embrace the SOULFIRE, your innate talents, connections, and influencer status will surface. Success follows when you listen to your SOULFIRE.

Yet many of us lose the birthright to our SOULFIRE because we unknowingly choose to mindlessly follow The OTHERS. Somewhere along the way we buy into the belief that our needs are pointless and the cause of The OTHERS is more noble, honorable, humble, caring, important, good. That good people put their wants aside for others.

SUCCESS FOLLOWS WHEN YOU LISTEN TO YOUR SOULFIRE.

People quote scripture backing this belief—where Jesus Christ says, "lay down your burdens, pick up your cross, and follow me."

"If anyone would come after me, let him deny himself and take up his cross and follow me. For whoever would save his life[a] will lose it, but whoever loses his life for my sake will find it. For what will it profit a man if he gains the whole world and forfeits his soul?"

*Matthew 16:24-26 English Standard Version (ESV)

Though, true, we have misinterpreted, and mis-taught the intent of this line for our personal betterment and societal manipulation. Christ was never asking us to follow an unknown person—The OTHERS. He never asked us to follow, do, or be something that goes against the root of our soul. Christ asked us to follow Him. Through His work He showed us and laid out all about who He was, all of what He stood for—as well as did not stand for— what our role is, and what the expectations of us are.

Christ asked us to find our truth in Him. He asked us to use our gifts to create connections. He asked us not to judge the differences, but to focus on the points of connection. He asked us to serve all of our needs: theirs and ours (Mark 12:30-31.) Here you learn that your needs should be first after your DIVINE PARTNERSHIP so that you can bring your best to the rest of the world.

He asked us to buck the social norms like He did. Because flipping tables in the temple was quite rebellious back in the day (Matthew 21:12-13); He taught us to be successful through service. Christ asked us to take all that we do— from the words that we speak to the actions we take—and make them matter, to ensure we not waste a moment of our earthly life. He asked us to find, live, and be our IT— our SOULFIRE.

LEARN.
Being your best is a service to the world not for yourself.

DO.
Take time to mull over what truly defines your Soulfire for you.

BELIEVE.
Never forget that how you see the world is a unique gift given solely to you.

BECOME.
Clarity is Divinity. Refine yourself so that you are clear about who you are with yourself and the world.

CONNECT.
Take time to understand what your SOULFIRE is for you. Tap into resources like Soulfire Life and my weekly podcasts: *Soulfire Life and Success Rebel* to learn how to discover the depth of your Divine purpose.

48

Chapter 8

WHY YOUR DESIRE TO BE KNOWN MATTERS (AND IS A GOOD THING)

MAY YOU FULLY RECOGNIZE YOUR POWER AND PURPOSE THAT IS WITHIN.

Let's be honest.

When you see the word "notoriety" what is your gut reaction?

For most people it is, "not me."

I am not "noteworthy." I am not prideful, ego driven, or narcissistic—to dare claim notoriety is lunacy. I know my place and that's not it.

Really?

Why?

THE WEALTH IN WORDS.

When you look at the root of the word, notoriety, you see synonyms such as: well known, fame, renown, celebrity, favor, in the state of being generally or publicly known, and a wide recognition for one's deeds.

Don't you want grace, favor, to be known for something good?

Don't you want people to trust you, believe in you, look up to you, know that you have their back?

Of course, you do, and none of that is "bad" when your intention is good.

You see, most people's SOULFIRE has nothing to do with them. They are merely the hands and feet. You too, are merely the hands and feet of the greater purpose for your existence.

I like how the ancient Greeks and Romans looked at creativity. To them it was a spirit that came and visited people until it found a person who said, "yes" to partnering together.

Yes, a partnership between you and creativity. Think about all of the amazing masterpieces that were created back then and still stand today: the Arch of Constantine, the Parthenon, the Temple of Athena Nike, and the Acropolis.

Ironically, we did not see the mad artist story becoming part of the human consciousness until our societal views shifted to the gift of creativity being within the artist—not a partnership with something greater than themselves.

I believe the same holds true with you relative to living your dreams; to having success your way. We may use pronouns like "you" and "yours," but it isn't us. We are just the hands and feet, the spokesperson—if you will—for the Divine, behind the scenes guy.

I believe something similar is asked to occur between us and the Divine. Will you partner together with the vision of your soul—your SOULFIRE?

So, when we shy away from the word "notoriety" or "success"—claiming it has no meaning on our life, we push off, deny the Divine influence, and begin to focus on us.

Because yes, solo, without listening to our Divine SOULFIRE, who are we? Nothing much more than a really good doer—and The OTHERS know it. That's why there are so many social stories around being humble, not being prideful, diminishing ego, success, money, and power.

OUR SPIRITUAL NATURE HAS BEEN WARPED.

We have been taught lies about what it means to be humble, to live a life of success, to be financially affluent, and to devote your life to your dreams.

THOSE ACTIONS DON'T TAKE YOU AWAY FROM YOUR DIVINE CALLING, THEY BRING YOU TO IT.

Being bold enough to live a life of success and notoriety, or as I like to say, NEW NOTORIETY, means that you are in flow, partnership with the Divine and your purpose.

BECAUSE WHEN YOU ACKNOWLEDGE YOUR PARTNER OF INSPIRATION, AND YOU CHOOSE TO PLAY YOUR PART AS THE HANDS AND FEET OF THE OPERATION, A LIFE FAVOR, GRACE, INFLUENCE, SUCCESS, AND AFFLUENCE COMES.

Not because of who you are but because of what your DIVINE PARTNERSHIP means on the cosmic stage.

LEARN.

The desires of your heart aren't a solo act. This is a soul partnership. Through this perspective you can see how your dreams can be a reality when you acknowledge your Divine purpose and partner.

DO.

Take back the words that light you on fire and stir your heart. Social perception of words doesn't matter if they stir your soul.

BELIEVE.

You are fully capable of having every single dream come to pass because you are not alone in the creation.

BECOME.

Be clear in your heart and mind what this DIVINE PARTNERSHIP means so that you don't fall into society's belief of solo success.

CONNECT.

Connect with the true blessing your SOULFIRE is. It is a DIVINE PARTNERSHIP and fulfillment to your soul, and you are blessed enough to live, work, and breathe the earthly benefits

54

Chapter 9

WHAT ARE YOU REALLY CAPABLE OF

MAY YOU FOREVER REALIZE THE UNENDING DEPTH OF BRILLIANCE THAT LIES INSIDE OF YOU.

We all come out of the womb with desires. And though they may look very primitive, such as the desire for food. The truth is we are born with unseen, transformational desires as well, such as love, connection, and certainty.

As brand-new souls to this side of Heaven, we are unable to fully or logically articulate the desires of our heart. But the Heavenly desires we are born with are still there.

We rely on the people around us to connect with us not just physically, but on a heart-to-heart, soul-to-soul level. So that they feel the deeper unspoken desires of what we are searching for.

Yes, that is good parenting 101.

FAILURE TO THRIVE.

We see studies time and time again, which show that when babies and young children under the age of two years old only receive the outward desires such as food, but fail to receive the unarticulated, deeper desires of their heart—they fail to thrive, grow, create relationships, or give back to this world in a meaningful manner.

Failure to thrive isn't just an affliction that affects our young, it can affect all of us. We know from experience that failure to thrive with the elderly is an ever-growing concern as relationships, communication, and contact gets limited either by illness or institutions. We also learn that personal contact, stimulation, and connection are the roots of what make us human.

These desires—spoken and unspoken—never leave us.

We are taught by The OTHERS that whatever you can articulate, whatever is logical. are the only things worthy of investing in. All else doesn't or shouldn't exist.

You are made to believe your dreams, heartfelt desires, a yearning for something more, better, to transform, make a difference, matter on a deeper level—none of that is real. Those are fairy tales that no logical, rational, mature adult would even bother with.

Yet they aren't.

BORN CAPABILITIES.

The unseen, transformational desires we are born with are always there. Our SOULFIREs are inside of us—waiting for us to recognize, acknowledge, and begin to fan the flames through our action so that this deep soul-filled desire can be met, and the true transformational work of our lives can begin.

It doesn't matter that or how The OTHERS have tried to destroy you and your dreams. Their abortion-like tactics to miseducate, deny the truth of what your dreams really are, or make you feel like you are going to miss out if you keep dreams and desires will work.

YOUR DREAMS, YOUR SOULFIRE, AREN'T TAKEN AWAY—YOU CHOOSE TO CUT OUT, BURN ALIVE, AND DISMEMBER THE DIVINE GIFT YOU SEEK.

Simply because you allow The OTHERS to plant seeds of fear, doubt, and not fitting in.

From the media to our educational system, this dream aborting approach surrounds us. Many of us fall for their tactics and many regret our decisions...a little too late.

But just like with abortions, some of our dreams are still born alive.

OUR DIVINE FIGHTER SPIRIT COULD NOT BE DESTROYED BY THE OTHERS.

And in such instances, we are told, what is done is done. You can't save your dreams.

The "humane" thing to do is to put our Divine nature, our Divinely planted uniqueness, in a stainless steel basin off in an empty room, while it screams in pain; it screams for your heart, screams for your touch, your safety, your hands, your actions, and your energy. All the while, as you are being told to forget about it, move on, what is done is done—you quietly adapt to the mass mentality and do as you are told.

But it isn't.

You can make the wrong choice. You can have a moment of mental weakness where The OTHERS win.

YOU CAN FOLLOW THEIR LOGIC FOR A TIME, YET YOU CAN STILL CHOOSE DIFFERENTLY.

You can choose to go save your dreams. You can choose to go reverse the actions that were meant to kill your dreams—and you can breathe life back into them.

Because your dreams are more than yours. They are Divine.

YOUR DREAMS, YOUR DESIRES, YOUR SOUL'S PURPOSE, WERE NOT FORMED ON THIS SIDE OF HEAVEN, THEREFORE THE LAWS OF MAN, THE LAWS OF THE OTHERS, HAVE NO EFFECT ON YOUR ABILITY TO LIVE, BE AND PROSPER FROM YOUR SOULFIRE.

The only way your Divine nature and the possibilities it brings never produce the harvest and impact they were meant to is because you choose not to.

Your age, income, education, race, sex, gender, or health status doesn't matter. The Divine possibilities you are born with will always be there inside of you on some level. Even if you believed the lies of The OTHERS. Even if you tried to cut every ounce of your dreams out of you, some remain. It is your task to:

Find those pieces.

Locate those little embers.

Begin to send them love.

Begin to think about it.

Begin to care about it.

Begin to breathe your energy into what is there.

These are your Divine dreams. This is Divinely appointed influence, success, and notoriety you are going for.

It doesn't matter that The OTHERS think they have won. The One who created you in your mother's womb. The One who took your daddy's sperm and momma's egg and literally made a spark happen at the moment of your conception. You can take those pieces that remain of your SOULFIRE and regrow the reach, regrow the influence, accelerate the grace and favor on the outward actions you take.

Your partnership, and the possibilities it brings, are not over. It is never over until you say so. You aren't partnered with a man.

YOU ARE PARTNERED SOLELY WITH THE DIVINE IN A UNIQUE WAY THAT ONLY YOU AND HE CAN COMPLETE. HE IS WILLING AND ABLE. YOU ARE ALWAYS ABLE. THE QUESTION IS ARE YOU WILLING.

LEARN.

Just because you have denied the callings of your heart, your SOULFIRE, your entire life up until now. You still have time to take action.

DO.

Take conscious effort daily to connect with others, stimulate your heart, and have meaningful physical contact with those you love and who love you. Even if it is your furry four-legged family member.

BELIEVE.

You are no accident. The spark that formed you is still there. Never forget the Divine spark is still inside of you.

BECOME.

Rebels are warriors. You must be willing to fight for your heart, the people you are meant to be of service to and for your DIVINE PARTNERSHIP.

CONNECT.

The truth is that it is all possible. Connect with that truth. Breathe it and believe it—until you know in every ounce of your being that your SOULFIRE is possible through you and with you.

Chapter 10

THE "WHAT IFS" OR A WINNING LIFE

MAY YOUR MIND BE DIVINELY FOCUSED SOLELY ON THE DREAMS OF YOUR HEART.

Growing up, many kids love to play the game of "why." If you have kids, you know this all too well. You will be driving down the road in the car and all you hear is

"Why is the sky blue, Mom?"

"Why do dogs bark, Dad?"

"Why do I have to be nice to my little sister?"

"Why do I need to go to school?"

"Why do I have to eat my vegetables?"

OUR HUMAN NATURE MAKES US CURIOUS BEINGS AND OUR HUMAN NATURE IS NATURALLY POSITIVE.

Yep, we come out of the womb knowing, feeling, and being love. Our brain is hardwired for only love.

If human beings were defined by one emotion, love would be it. We need to feel love from the inside out and from the outside in. Neuroscience research is even beginning to discover that our addiction crisis is actually due to the brain misinterpreting a tragic event and viewing the "high" as love.

Babies don't know anything other than love—until life's experiences teach them to be fearful and anxious. Fear is not an emotion we come into this world with. We learn it. And who do we learn it from? The OTHERS.

As adults, we turn our curious nature from "why" into "what if'."

OUR MINDSET ROOTED IN DIVINE LOVE IS TRANSFORMED INTO A MIND CONTROLLED BY THE FEAR OF THE OTHERS.

"What if I fail?"

"What if that person doesn't like me?"

"What if this client leaves me?"

"What if I gain weight, lose my hair, get more wrinkles?"

We question the possibilities of being able to live up to the success markers woven into the social stories The OTHERS say matter. We focus our attention, energy, and actions on the shiny objects to the left and right. We fail to look at our heart and the gift of our unique SOULFIRE, which stands straight in front of us.

We fail to acknowledge our beautiful gifts because no one else is touting its beauty.

We see the potential. We feel the connection. We see the beauty.

BUT BECAUSE EVERYONE ELSE IS IGNORING IT LIKE THE ABORTED DREAM THEY SEE IT, AS WE DO: THE SAME.

We believe that because if The OTHERS don't see the value of our SOULFIRE then clearly there is nothing worthy there.

WHAT IF.

But, what if we choose to believe the beauty we see standing right in front of us?

What if we choose to say—not just with our mouths—
that originality is key? Instead, what if we show
with our actions and energy we believe our SOULFIRE
of originality is valuable, worthy, beautiful,
powerful, influential, and noteworthy.

What if we trusted our hearts more than the skewed
logic The OTHERS put into our heads?

What if we knew from our deepest core that the
Divine love born inside of us and the dreams,
desires, status, creation, manifestation, and
transformation, which comes with it matters more
than anything else on this planet? Not just to you,
but also to every single sentient being you meet
from the day you enter this side of Heaven to the
moment you return.

OUR "WHAT IFS" AND "WHYS" ARE POWERFUL TOOLS BECAUSE THEY ARE DIVINELY PLACED.

And just like with the possibilities of our dreams,
we can take the power of our "what ifs" and "whys,"
and turn them into our success driven advantage.

We can choose to "why" every aspect of the way we
live, think, exist, and behave.

We can choose to "why" our relationships, time,
intentions, motives, purposes, dreams, and goals.

Or, we can choose differently if the answers to our
"why" don't stir our soul, set our hearts on fire, or
fan the flames of SOULFIRE inside of us.

We can reconnect, with a mind of love, and see the "what ifs" in our lives as the hopeful possibilities they are. We just need to ask the important questions:

- What if I succeed?

- What if I influence generations?

- What if my Divine work springboards the people around me into their Divine paths and lives of NEW NOTORIETY?

- What if all of this is greater than me?

- What if this was never about me?

- What if it has always been about a deeper divine message weaving the planes of the earth and Divine in a way that I am not consciously aware of?

- What if the life of NEW NOTORIETY, for which my SOULFIRE sets me up is bigger, better, and far more influential, and successful than I could ever imagine?

THOUGH OUR "WHAT IFS" AND "WHYS" SEEM LIKE QUESTIONS ROOTED IN CHILDLIKE INNOCENCE, THE TRUTH REMAINS: THESE ARE THE QUESTIONS THAT CREATE THE VERY ANSWERS, WHICH CHANGE OUR TRAJECTORY.

And just like with everything else, we can choose if the trajectory is for our good or the perceived good of The OTHERS.

LEARN.

Love is your natural state. When you work, speak, or react out of anything less than love you are out of your DIVINE PARTNERSHIP.

DO.

Set your phone alarm or reminder in your schedule for a quick "90 Second Check In" with yourself every 90 minutes. This will keep you on track and in love. Go to http://successrebelbook.com for your digital copy of the *Success Rebel Go Guide*.

BELIEVE.

That asking "why" is the way to rediscover your true heart.

BECOME.

Consciously return to being love obsessed. Choose to find love in everything you do, in every experience life presents you, and in every interaction. We must reprogram our brains back to their original love filled state.

CONNECT.

It is essential for our human nature to be in an environment that allows us to feel love from the inside out. Make a conscious effort to find these moments in your everyday life—or seek out online communities, like our Success Rebel Society, to get the love filled goodness you need.

Chapter 11

POWER OF POSSIBILITIES

MAY YOU NEVER FORGET THE CREATOR OF THE UNIVERSE IS THE CREATOR OF YOU.

There is the wide standing belief that a glass is either half full or half empty. This simple test is designed to measure how you organically see situations. Are you naturally more optimistic or a bit more pessimistic?

These are the parameters and limiters that The OTHERS present. And because you are given only option A and option B instinctually those are the only two options you see.

This truth, like most social stories from The OTHERS, is flawed. The glass is neither.

In actuality the glass is full. Part liquid that we see and part air/ gas that we do not see. But if we see it or not, it is still there. Complete and whole in every way. The glass doesn't need more water or less. It is perfect the way it is.

Yet, we don't intuitively view it as such simply by the question posed to us by The OTHERS. Our human minds are easily framed. Give people two options: they intuitively think there are only two options from which to choose. And it is this limiter that The OTHERS constantly rely on when it comes to the possibilities inside of you.

How much money can you make in a month, this, or that?

Will your marriage last, yes, or no?

Do you want fries or a salad with your meal?

Yes, on some level we need limiters because without them our minds would constantly be in a state of "what if." But we need those limiters based on the possibilities we hold in our hearts and not limiters set by social protocol.

Possibilities don't have to be logical or logistical. Your success partner and true gifting is not from this world. Don't let someone tell you that it isn't possible to make $750,000 per year, per month, per day, per minute.

IF YOU KNOW THAT THE NUMBER, GOAL, INFLUENCE, RELATIONSHIP, OR NOTORIETY YOU SEEK IS DIVINELY ROOTED NOT EGO DRIVEN, THEN WHAT YOU SEEK IS POSSIBLE.

ASK AND TAKE ACTION.

The next line you usually hear is about believing and receiving. If you just believe hard enough then you will have it. Receiving the possibilities, you are meant for isn't like taking a poop. You don't believe hard enough—and by hook or crook—poof, there is what you have been looking for. We aren't, after all, Golden Geese laying golden eggs everywhere.

To truly live a life of success and NEW NOTORIETY—a life filled with possibilities—you have to be raw and honest about the limiters you naturally put on situations, people, income, possibilities.

BECAUSE IT DOESN'T MATTER WHAT THE DIVINE HAS IN STORE FOR YOU IF YOU HAVE ALREADY LIMITED THE POTENTIAL OF THE POSSIBILITIES.

Similar to the example of the glass, believing and receiving is really one of: Ask and Take Action. You have to learn how to ask and take action. Asking and action are a balance that many of us struggle with. We are normally good at one but not so graceful with the other. Meaning that we look like a first-time driver trying to shift a standard car into gear. We do it, but it isn't pretty nor done right all the time.

Most people looking to have their lives matter in a significant and successful way tend to be very good at the take action part. They understand that they are the hands and feet of their DIVINE PARTNERSHIP.

BUT IF ALL WE DO IS TAKE ACTION; WE ARE ALWAYS ALONE.

Our partner can never fully supply their resources, share their connections or insights to help us and help the overall work of the SOULFIRE if we don't ask first and then take action. Yes, we allow ourselves to be limited in ways we rarely see the full depth of the ramifications or if we do, it is solely in retrospect.

LEARN.

Very few true limiters in life exist. The majority of the time there is always a solution to every situation. You just have to believe and search for the possibilities.

DO.

Begin to see the full truth of the situation at hand, not just the limiting scope people are pointing you towards.

BELIEVE.

You have not because you ask not. People, the Divine, and other forces unseen want to help you. Be vulnerable and ask for what you feel you need—be it something from this side of Heaven or the other: Ask and Take Action.

BECOME.

Be solution—not compromised—focused. There is a solution to every problem that leads everyone to feel like a successful winner. Don't fall for the old line that everything in life is a compromise. Be living proof that every situation has a success-filled solution.

CONNECT.

It is easy to lose sight of your grandness in the vastness of the universe. Take time daily to remind yourself and connect with the truth that the God who created the vast galaxies also chose you. You are valuable. You have a purpose. You are loved beyond measure and you are meant to love beyond measure.

2

YOU MUST MASTER SUCCESS, STRUGGLE, AND SEX

Chapter 12

THE CIRCUS OF LIFE

MAY YOUR SOUL ALWAYS LIVE FREE NO MATTER WHERE YOU MAY BE.

We come out of the womb as fighters. Some of us are vocal, others more mellow, but we instinctively take life on, and get our needs met in our unique way. As time progresses our instincts can get overshadowed by our environment, social stories, and the energy that surrounds us. And as the fighters that we are, we course correct, modify, adjust, and keep going.

Doesn't that sound like a healthy way to live? Your terms, adjusting as you need, but never compromising on your end goal?

If we instinctively get "how to live life," why is it that as we grow and evolve we lose our direction, values, and unique perspective?

That's where The OTHERS come in.

THE Others SEEM BENIGN IN THE BEGINNING.
LITTLE ASKS, LITTLE NUDGES THAT TURN INTO
PUSHES AND ASKS THAT TURN INTO THE
PROVERBIAL FULL ON MELTDOWN IF THEY
DON'T GET THEIR WAY.

- Why won't you allow this strange person to be alone with your child?
- Well, they are old. So, it's ok if they berate you. They are your senior after all.
- Why won't you hug your co-workers? We are like family after all.
- You don't want to attend the optional business party after work on Friday.
- Well, all the other parents are wearing the team gear to show support to the kids. You don't want to be left out, do you?
- It is only nice to invite long lost cousin Bob to your intimate wedding. Don't you love your family?
- They didn't mean what they said or did, or how they behaved. You should just give them a break.

The OTHERS are all around us; it is hard to escape.
No matter, everywhere you turn there they are.
There is no place to hide, to rest, to recoup, to

remind yourself of your SOULFIRE you once felt so clearly. And because The OTHERS have long been at this game of suppression they know exactly how to use the people and things you love the most to their advantage.

ARE YOU WILLING TO LOSE IT ALL?

When I had just turned 20 years old, I thought the world was my oyster. I had a job I loved, Dean's list in school every semester, had a man I adored, and the cutest sun filled condo, which I shared with my then 18-year-old cat, Socks, and my two ferrets, Pike and Ludwig.

Honestly, everything felt perfect. Life felt exciting, lovely, and had a great flow to it.

Fast forward two years, I had gotten married. We moved from Connecticut back to my hometown in Louisiana, ending up in a house with toxic mold. Besides making me really sick and forever changing my life and health perspective, we lost everything. My then husband and I literally packed up my car with our cat and a few new clothing items we bought, and we left everything behind.

There is no cleaning your items. There is no saving it. If you don't want to bring any toxic mold spores with you to your next home, you leave everything behind. To abandon a home, career, my husband's medical practice, and all our earthly possessions at 23 years old was hard. I don't think I ever was a very material person, but truly having to leave everything behind, tests your limits.

Over my ten-year marriage, we ended up with three homes that had toxic mold in them. Every time we got smarter about what to ask about, look for, but The OTHERS played the card of people simply lying for their benefit and hopefully our demise.

I didn't fully understand how easily The OTHERS could manipulate people back then. But I did learn how things truly are just THINGS. Instead of pining for what was lost, the beautiful furnishings, homes, etc. I allowed the Divine to use this situation for me to realize that The OTHERS can no longer use possessions to stop me. As the Bible says, God used what the Devil meant for my harm for my good.

THE OTHERS TRIED TO SUPPRESS MY LIFE BY TRYING TO TAKE IT. WHEN THEY COULDN'T DO THAT, THEY TRIED TO TAKE ALL MY THINGS.

THE TEST OF ALL TESTS.

But it isn't just people that you don't really know whom The OTHERS use for their bidding. They also use some of the closest people to you.

Since my divorce I have had one serious relationship. This guy checked all of the boxes on so many levels. We were in sync in ways I had never had with another human being. We both loved that neither one of us was looking for that "typical" relationship. We both had successful careers and we wanted to see each other thrive in the areas of life outside of us.

I truly thought this guy was "the one" until about three and half years into our relationship.

At that time, we both had hit stressful patches in our careers. And he had the added stress of his kids. Instead of supporting each other with our stress, I felt he retreated from the relationship. I felt like if everything wasn't perfect in my life, if I shared any struggle I might be going through that he viewed that as overwhelming and retreated even more.

The mindset The OTHERS tried to implant—that people only want me if I am perfect—had me for a brief second.

Stress can damage any relationship. Factor in a long-distance relationship and that combination can mean death. But I am Scorpio loyal. So, if you are "my" person I will do whatever it takes to make you happy and keep our relationship together. Remember, there is a solution to every situation—if you are willing to find it.

Thank goodness, I quickly recognized the deceptive thought The OTHERS were trying to embed and activate in my mind and soul. Because I recognized what was happening to us, I went in for one of those tough conversations. I went into this call with no doubt we and this relationship were going to leave this call intact and better than ever. Well, by the end of this call our four-year relationship was over.

It wasn't that harsh words were said. It wasn't that we didn't love each other anymore. It was simply because The OTHERS had a hold on him that he could not see and didn't want to see. If he couldn't see it for himself he surely could not see how that hold was limiting him—and trying to kill me.

The most ironic thing about that breakup was the timing. In that month, The OTHERS just didn't go after the love of my life, they went after my money through a frivolous lawsuit, and my SOULFIRE by manipulating long time staff members to leave with no notice and steal company assets on their way out the door.

THIS AIN'T A RODEO—IT'S A DAMN CIRCUS.

You see, The OTHERS know it takes time to break the will of a child, teenager, optimistic young adult. Throw enough crap, shame, rejection, or failure their way and most people will choose to surrender to the path of alleged safety, security, and The OTHERS version of success. It is never one test, it is the same test multiple times, by multiple people that The OTHERS bring your way.

You see The OTHERS have been at this game long before your soul entered this world. They have their plans and tricks. They know how to get you to see life from their perspective and not your own.

THE OTHERS ARE CUNNING.

They find what matters most to you: whether it be family, love, acceptance, or connection—whichever one of the fundamental humans needs you innately desire. Then they do whatever they can to remove it from your life and hold it hostage until you obey.

YES, THE OTHERS TREAT YOU LIKE A WILD CIRCUS ANIMAL, WHICH NEEDS TO BE TAMED AND PLAY ITS ROLE, SO THAT THEY MAKE THE MONEY. YOU SIMPLY EXIST.

And though that sounds horrible—for you and the circus animal—we all do it to various levels every day. From obeying an outdated dress code rule to playing a social role that doesn't fit our SOULFIRE, intentions, or version of success.

The act of suppression from The OTHERS is designed to have you lose focus on your SOULFIRE while pacifying the one human need you desire most. Their old school approach of suppression was the "good ol 'boys club." Saying women were lesser, and once again distorting the message of Jesus Christ when it comes to money, women, relationships, marriage, intelligence, duties, etc.

Their approach has done a job that honestly is the most brilliant mental warfare tactics since the *Art of War* by Sun Tzu back in 500 BC. Now that many people are consciously aware of the suppressive game at play, we don't blame the game maker, The

OTHERS. We don't even investigate the truth of the information they told us. Instead we take malice with the alleged root of all of the suppression, men, Christianity, and our leaders.

As the belief and value in men and Jesus Christ begin to wane, The OTHERS put into overdrive their ultimate act of confusion—the idea that none of us know who or what we are—period. And should you identify with anything previously supported and praised by The OTHERS, such as traditional gender roles, identity, or simply not engaging, etc., the next step is to convince you that you are basically wrong.

Yes, The OTHERS are trying to take away the SOULFIRE we are born with so that our indoctrination to their circus suppression happens sooner.

GONE ARE THE DAYS OF REBELLIOUS KIDS AND TEENS—THE CONFORMITY IS UNDERWAY UNDER THE GUISE OF HONEST TRUTH.

But in reality all that is happening is that we are losing our way from the Divine path that is created uniquely for us. We spin our wheels playing the next level of the suppressive games The OTHERS have created. We don't use our energy, brilliance, and Divine perspective in a manner that positively impacts the world. We don't create the success and influence we desire. We don't develop the relationships and experiences that would truly satisfy our innate human needs. Therefore, we never achieve the financial success we long for.

THOUGH THE NEW GAME THE OTHERS HAVE DEVISED MAY FEEL LIKE FREEDOM, IT IS ACTUALLY MORE DANGEROUS THAN ANY OTHER VERSION OF SOCIETAL SUPPRESSION EVER PLAYED.

In the end the outcome is still the same.

WE HAVE THE MASS MAJORITY OF PEOPLE FEELING LOST, BEAT UP, TRUSTING NO ONE, UNCLEAR WHY THEY CAN'T SUCCEED, WONDERING WHY THEY HAVE DREAMS AND DESIRES THAT SEEM SO "WRONG" WHEN VIEWED AGAINST THE SOCIETAL STANDARDS THE OTHERS HAVE HAILED AS GOOD.

Which in the end takes your wild, beautiful, Divine ways and turns you into a well-trained circus act with an even smaller cage than before. And we all know what happens in the end to a caged, wild, and unhappy animal—they escape or die trying.

LEARN.

A one-time choice to step into your SOULFIRE and DIVINE PARTNERSHIP isn't going to keep The OTHERS at bay. Their attacks will increase, and they will force you to decide you or them.

DO.

Write your intentions for every action you take— even small ones. When you write out your heart-purpose, in that moment you create a more powerful experience for you and all who are involved, and you will also keep yourself focused should The OTHERS try to mess with you.

And if that feels a bit overwhelming, don't worry. I have shared with you a copy of my daily planner so that you, too can stay clear about your intentions on everything you do. The *Success Rebel Go Guide* is available for free at http://SuccessRebelBook.com

BELIEVE.

Never forget that you, your SOULFIRE, your DIVINE PARTNERSHIP —all of this matters.

BECOME.

Begin to take steps back in those difficult conversations. Discernment is key to understanding why the flow isn't happening in a particular situation. Is it because your intentions are mismatched? It is because you have a social story that is limiting you from seeing the truth. Or The OTHERS are at play in a bigger way. Taking a mental, emotional, spiritual, and sometimes physical step back from a situation is the key to build up your ability to properly discern what is truly happening.

CONNECT.

Though it is human nature to want and need physical, emotional, and spiritual connection, you have to learn how to connect first with yourself, your SOULFIRE, and DIVINE PARTNERSHIP. Because these are three connections that The OTHERS can never take away from you—unless you choose to abandon them.

Chapter 13

THE TRUE HEART OF THE MATTER

MAY YOU ALWAYS KNOW THAT YOUR HEART IS YOUR GREATEST ASSET.

As a society we are taught to associate our hearts with love. And though this social story has served us well. The current en vogue story around the heart is that it is simply a functional piece of anatomy with no emotional tie to life as we know it.

Did you know that:

- The heart remains in a constant two-way communication with your brain.

- Studies have proven that using positive emotion focused tools can significantly help improve the health, wellbeing, and physical ailments with

some of the most debilitating chronic
conditions.

- The heart is the body's most powerful rhythmic
  magnetic field and that this field can be
  detected by people and with sensitive
  instruments.

- And that the emotions that we feel don't just
  affect our heart's rhythm but our cells as well.

What I have seen, in working for over two decades
with entrepreneurs, and have personally
experienced is that it is one thing to identify your
SOULFIRE. However, to live it, to truly be those hands
and feet—you need not just love but heart.

HEART AND LOVE.

Most people don't distinguish the difference
between heart and love. Love is an emotion, a
feeling, an energetic experience. But our hearts are
strong, have structures, systems, and regulations
that work 24/7/365. There is no conscious thought
needed to make the systems of the heart work. But
you can consciously create the emotion of love.

When it comes to being a Success Rebel, living your
dreams and life of NEW NOTORIETY, both are needed
for success. You need LOVE in the sense of passion,
enthusiasm, and drive. And you need HEART in the
sense of the never stopping, perfectly functioning,
never growing tired, machines that our hearts are.

Because we tend to equate the heart with the caricature shape that we see plastered all over the grocery store around Valentine's Day. We fail to see the beauty that is the heart.

- The heart is the size of your adult fist.
- The sound of the heart beating is made by the opening and closing of valves.
- Your heart beats around 100,000 times per day.
- The heart has its own electrical supply and can beat independently from the body.
- Your heart is considered the strongest muscle in the human body because it can beat over three billion times in your lifetime.
- And many of the greatest philosophers and spiritual leaders have theorized that while we are alive the soul resides in the heart chakra area.

It is our responsibility and ability to create such a structure for our lives, to support our SOULFIRE — that Divine "IT." A structure that allows all of the blessings, favor, grace, influence, and notoriety to build up our lives not tear them down.

WHICH CELEBRITY ARE YOU?

We have all heard stories of two relatively identical celebrities. Similar in age, industry, talent, financially and perceived success. One is able to keep growing, evolve, transform, and find new ways to share and express their Divinely gifted partnership. Alternatively, we hear of how the other celebrity begins to self-destruct, becomes financially unstable, and sadly...no longer sought after or considered influential.

What's the difference between the two celebrities?

The structure around their Divine gifting necessary for them to execute, be the hands and feet of the partnership, while building up their life. Without continued support, it all falls apart.

Here is why.

The idea of consistency sounds exhausting. The OTHERS teach us that there is no way anyone, let alone little ol' you, can handle doing anything continuously.

Think about your lack of freedom?

What if you get tired?

What if you change your mind?

What if you get bored?

What if it is no longer fun?

Committing to something that is a lifelong, continuous choice, is so patriarchal.

YET THAT CONTINUOUS CONSISTENT COMMITMENT IS THE ONLY WAY THE SUCCESS YOU SEEK HAPPENS.

It is the only way the life of NEW NOTORIETY that you truly desire happens.

YOUR SOULFIRE ISN'T SOME THROW AWAY FASHION.

This is a partnership between you and the One who created you. Commitment is key.

THE DIVINE FLOW.

JUST LIKE WITH YOUR PHYSICAL HEART— WHERE THE DIVINE EFFORTLESSLY PROVIDES FOR US THROUGHOUT OUR ENTIRE LIVES THIS SIDE OF HEAVEN, HE DOES THE SAME FOR OUR SOULFIRES IF WE LET HIM.

But just like today's modern medicine, we can intervene in the Divine and try to take over the flow of our SOULFIRE. And just like with modern medicine, the Divine simply does it better.

As with our hearts, there is a natural ebb and flow that happens. The same holds true with the structure of your Divine gifting. The idea of exhaustion is a simple illusion The OTHERS use to deter you from following your dreams.

Growing up I always wanted to be a heart surgeon. I knew I could never be a veterinarian because I like animals too much —but cutting open people and repairing their hearts seemed A-Okay to me.

The physical structure of the heart has such a mechanical beauty to it. It is raw, a bit messy, but so unique in its design that its shape is no accident. Simply put, four chambers, three layers, and valves make this masterpiece work.

When we look at this simplified outline of the structure of the heart, we see the Divine's repeated patterns and proof of how our SOULFIRE flows and how DIVINE PARTNERSHIP works.

Let's start with the three layers of the heart muscle itself. These three layers play similar roles to three aspects of NEURO HUMAN BRANDING.

- The epicardium is the protector layer similar to our biological aspects in NEURO HUMAN BRANDING, primal, functional, and strong.

- The myocardium is the layer of muscle inside the heart. Similar to our subconscious mind and how it is the main worker in our lives.

- Lastly we have the endocardium. This muscle actually lines the valves and chambers. It is the "how and when things flow" part of the heart. And that is exactly how social stories work in our lives and relationships.

The coolest part of the heart to me are the chambers. We have two receivers, the atrium chambers, and two givers... the ventricle chambers. I find it highly fascinating that we have to receive not once, but twice before we give. Before the flow can truly happen.

This is precisely how the flow of your SOULFIRE and DIVINE PARTNERSHIP work if you want to have the influence, grace, reach, and life of NEW NOTORIETY. You have to pause enough to receive not just once, but twice. You must receive first. It isn't "giving" first. It is "receiving" first.

THEN YOU ONLY GIVE AS MUCH AS YOU RECEIVE.

There is no over giving, bonusing, special deals here. To stay in Divine flow, it must be equal parts receiving as giving. It is from receiving the gift of your SOULFIRE, that influence and grace are given to the people you serve.

LEARN.

Just like your heart, you are strong and beautiful.
You have a unique flow and system that is Divinely
yours. True success, influence, and reach will
happen once you choose to discover and work in
your unique flow.

DO.

Take time to discover the love and heart you have
for your SOULFIRE.

BELIEVE.

You have the strength and the resilience to fully
achieve, live, and appreciate all that your SOULFIRE
creates —no matter what anyone else says.

BECOME.

Don't just set intentions for what you want out of
every task, situation, or experience. Consciously
choose how you want your heart to show up as well
as how you want your love to show in those
moments.

CONNECT.

You have to unlearn our modern ways of The
OTHERS. And begin to trust in the Divine flow that
God so effortlessly does for your hearts daily. You
have to trust that His Divine ways reach to your
partnership and SOULFIRE work. Create a small
group or join our Society so that you can track how
God comes through for you every time as you reset
your workflow from solo you to your DIVINE
PARTNERSHIP.

Chapter 14

WHY YOU MUST FIRST BE HAPPY TO BE SUCCESSFUL

MAY YOU ALWAYS REMEMBER THAT YOUR VOICE IS YOURS. NO ONE CONTROLS IT, BUT YOU.

Human beings are, quite honestly, really simple creatures. We simply want to be happy. Every single one of the six fundamental needs laid out in Human Needs Psychology are for our ultimate happiness.

Why happiness and not some other virtue?

Happiness covers everything.

If I am happy, I am loved.

If I am happy, I am accepted.

If I am happy, I am wanted.

If I am happy, I am desired.

If I am happy, I am sought after.

If I am happy I will have financial security.

If I am happy, I will enjoy how I spend my time.

If I am happy, I will be contributing.

If I am happy, I will be giving back.

If I am happy, I will have some level of influence in life and my relationships.

Happiness and success very much go hand in hand in how we view life.

THE DEATH OF HAPPINESS.

Yet, for us to have success and in turn, happiness, we have to be willing to go against the beliefs and limitations The OTHERS tout as virtues. In today's modern society the biggest virtue that The OTHERS promote, but is killing your success and happiness, is the moral platform of political correctness.

As with everything The OTHERS introduce, the original core belief sounds logical and "nice." Basically, be aware of what you say and who you say it to. This way people can hear the heart of your message and not the social story that comes with certain language.

Interestingly, political correctness was designed to tell us what we all know instinctively. That is to be a decent human being and not a selfish dick. Or at least that is what the politically correct movement started out as.

Today, the barrage and hatefulness around what is and is not acceptable and by whom, when, and where keeps most people saying nothing. That is exactly what The OTHERS want.

IF YOU SAY NOTHING YOU CAN'T BE KNOWN, YOUR WORK CAN'T MATTER, AND THAT SPARK INSIDE OF YOU WILL EVENTUALLY LESSEN IF NOT GO OUT ALTOGETHER.

Plus, if you aren't speaking your truth one of two things happens:

- You begin to doubt yourself and in turn beat yourself up because clearly you must be a horrible person to not know how offensive you really are.

- You no longer speak your truth...in a way that eats you up on the inside.

- You begin to feel your heart slowly die because your unique perspective does not feel wanted, valued, appreciated, or loved.

YES, YOU CAN LITERALLY FEEL YOUR
HAPPINESS DIE INSIDE OF YOU ALL BECAUSE
THE OTHERS SAID, "YOU CAN'T SAY THAT."
HERE IS WHAT I KNOW FROM WORKING WITH
THOUSANDS OF PEOPLE ONE-ON-ONE OVER
THE YEARS: MOST OF US ARE NOT ASSHOLES.

Most of us want to have good relationships,
connections, and truth. Simply put...we just want a
happy, successful life. They don't want to stomp on
you, hurt you, offend you, or honestly deal with you
at all. They simply want to do life on their terms,
and you aren't even part of the equation.

But that isn't the culture promoted on our media
outlets. We are not told about the decent folks who
just want to love life. Instead we are told about the
ministry to create more of a divide. And...because
this is the media message we receive, we all become
hypersensitive to the words the people around us
use. Needless to say, The OTHERS love it!

I have always been a bold talker, as my Mom would
say. I can remember when I was in the third grade
that I made the decision that no matter what, I was
going to tell it how I saw it. This way I wouldn't ever
have to worry about being caught in a lie. I wouldn't
ever have to worry about what I said behind
someone's back because I would know that whatever
I said I would have zero problems saying it to their
face. This is the exact way I have chosen to live my
life—third grade logic and all.

This perspective has made me a sought-after guest
for national media outlets because they like the raw

factor of my words. It has also created challenges, too. It wasn't until my then husband, did I ever care what people thought about my truth telling nature. And though my then husband loved it when it was directed towards other people, he was not the biggest fan of me using it on him and his shortcomings.

The OTHERS don't use people that you don't care about to make you conform. They use the ones you care about the most. This is exactly what happened with my then husband. He knew I wanted to make our marriage work and he knew I was working on becoming a better Christian woman and wife.

Because he was raised and "grew up" in the Church more than I, it was natural to discern to his discretion on matters like these. He knew it too.

I don't think he consciously was being malicious, but The OTHERS used him well to plant the seeds of doubt—to have me question my own motives, and to have me question the validity of my relationship with the Divine. I know it sounds moronic when you read it as written words on a page. How could a natural Success Rebel fall for one of the most basic tricks—love? That's exactly what got me!

During the years I did actively choose to edit myself, be more socially aligned, I lost myself. The natural flow of my SOULFIRE, work, and influence all slowly went away. What was once a steady stream becoming barely a trickle. At that time, I wouldn't have believed that simply being more PC with my language would have been the root of this loss, but it was.

It wasn't until years later...years after my divorce and sometimes in odd moments today that I realize the power we truly have with how we each uniquely see the world and express ourselves. I believe limiting it is more harmful than losing a limb because you ultimately lose the ability to share your heart.

THE SUCCESS REBEL WAY.

If you want to have the success of your dreams and live a life of NEW NOTORIETY, you have to be willing to risk being one of those people on the news being called out for not being PC.

- You have to be OK being lumped in the same news story with people who really are horrible jerks.

- You have to be willing to fight and defend the truth because that is the only way to achieve true success and happiness.

- You have to be OK with having outright lies told against you because the truth of who you are and what you are about doesn't fit The OTHERS' narrative.

And just like going after your SOULFIRE, saying, "Yes" to your DIVINE PARTNERSHIP, and living a life of NEW NOTORIETY—you don't just free yourself from the stronghold of The OTHERS when you refuse to play the PC game. You also loosen the strongholds this social story and entrapment has on everyone else around you.

BEING A SUCCESS REBEL REQUIRES YOU TO BE BOLD, MAKE THE FIRST MOVES, AND LEAD THE WAY.

In doing so you make it easier for the ones you love to be Success Rebels on their own terms, too.

LEARN.
What you say or don't say matters to your audience, but also to you. Don't limit your perspective simply because The OTHERS want you to.

Do.
Become aware of your thoughts and your words. See how often you choose to not say or edit yourself prior to you speaking. Recognize the "why" behind your self-editing and course adjust based on your motive.

BELIEVE.
Your unique, unedited perspective on the world is what the world needs.

BECOME.
Choose to unlearn the limiting communication patterns that The OTHERS have indoctrinated you into through the ideas of political correctness, where people who most matter to you ask you to tone down, or suggest your language choices are simply not "appropriate."

CONNECT.
Take the time to connect with your unique Divine perspective. Begin to journal, write, and then speak in an authentic manner to the SOULFIRE truth that lives inside of you.

Chapter 15

BEING GOOD AT SEX MAKES YOU GOOD AT BEING SUCCESSFUL

MAY YOU NEVER FORGET THAT INNOCENT SOUNDING DOESN'T MEAN INNOCENT INTENTIONS.

The two most taboo topics in most modern cultures are success and sex. That is by no accident.

Success and sex have been intertwined in biological, subconscious, and social levels since the beginning of time. Because if you do these two things successfully then you can control great wealth, influence, as well as the hearts and minds of the people. The OTHERS know this, and they can't let that happen.

CINDERELLA KILLED MY SEX LIFE.

Seemingly innocent social stories indoctrinating us before we were even born. We are spoon-fed Cinderella, Snow White, Alice In Wonderland, etc.

THESE ALLEGEDLY INNOCENT CHILDHOOD STORIES IMPLANT SUBCONSCIOUS LANDMINES THAT IF LEFT UNCHECKED CAN DESTROY OUR ABILITY TO BE SUCCESSFUL AT ANYTHING— BUSINESS, MONEY, RELATIONSHIPS, SEX—YOU NAME IT.

Mind you, The OTHERS are wicked smart! Stories are one of the ways we learn to model proper behavior. They are one of the few things we naturally remember as human beings. And because it is all under the guise of an innocent children's story, we willingly allow the ultimate bad magic trick to happen to us.

WE WANT TO BELIEVE IN THE HEART OF THE Others THE TRUTH OF THE STORY, AND THAT NOT EVERYTHING IN THIS WORLD IS DARK AND GRAY. FEW PEOPLE PAUSE AND ASK THEMSELVES "IS THIS REALLY INNOCENT?"

The truth is, however, that many of these "innocent" stories teach us the wrong message. Cinderella needs a fairy godmother to help make her look and be acceptable. She needs a Prince to find her and fix her mistakes. Her life is only going to turn around if the man is happy with her and chooses to save her.

Now the Prince doesn't get off easy in the story either. Even though he is the Prince, he doesn't even matter until the woman—aka Cinderella shows up. He has to find her, pursue her, and spend his hard-earned resources on a person he doesn't even know. By the time that is all done, and he actually does find her, it is only logical to make her his because he has invested so much into her and the relationship so far. It is just "smart" to keep going.

YES, FAIRYTALES ARE MIND F**KS.

Fairytales don't talk outright about success. Here is the gest of how success and life happen for us through the eyes of a fairytale.

Life doesn't happen until some outside force beyond your control says for it to.

It doesn't matter how hard you work, what your SOULFIRE is, or what type of DIVINE PARTNERSHIP you have.

You are told when and where.

Until that predetermined time—over which you have no control or say—you sit on the sidelines of life.

If you don't behave perfectly and impeccably complete a specific list of tasks that are unknown to you, all the good things, fun times, happiness will go away instantly to never return.

Doesn't that sound exactly how most people treat success?

Waiting for the magic fairy godmother's 'wand to say, "your turn." Knowing that if you don't do the dance right, or if your partner fails to play their part, your success will be taken from you instantly, and you will from now on forever be the evil step sister or brother in the story of your life?

DON'T BE LIKE GISELLE.

These stories seem innocent enough, but they create limiting patterns all throughout our life. From how we think dating should go to how to excel in our career. These stories don't just create expectations; they create a life pattern where you and I will walk out every single time— unless we wise up.

Over the years of teaching the SOULFIRE method and working with entrepreneurs on various aspects of being a Success Rebel, many "newbies" naively think that all of the tests, drama, social story triggers are outside of them.

They innocently, or being ego driven, believe that they are not the problem in their Success Rebel story. Clearly in the fairytales it is always someone else's' fault, that must be the case with me too. Wrong.

But then there are the leaders who have been on this Success Rebel journey for a bit. They know the buck stops with them. They are actively looking for the way out, the social story at play, the root to the game The OTHERS are trying to run.

Though progressive and powerful, this can easily lead to instant confusion. Over analyzing a situation without being grounded in your DIVINE PARTNERSHIP and clear about your own intentions in the moment can make the facts no longer look clear and get you into a loop of double mindedness. This leader loop reminds you of the Disney film *Enchanted*.

I am all too familiar with this storyline because I had a cat named, Cami, who loved hearing the music in this movie. So, here is the 150 word or less scoop.

Giselle is a beautiful maiden who goes to the castle to marry her Prince. Once at the castle she is so in love with love and doing the right thing her evil stepmom to be tricks her. Giselle falls into a well where she is banished to the place of no happy endings—New York City. Drama ensues as her Prince tries to locate her, save her, and they live happily ever after.

Giselle, like you, was so mentally caught up in doing the right thing, that she became dizzy in her own beliefs. It is easy for us to lose our grounding in the Divine and our SOULFIRE when we get so caught up making it happen that we, too get dizzy; we get overwhelmed, become anxious and fall down a well just like Giselle.

Learn.

You can't trust how people describe themselves or their work without being clear about their intentions first.

Do.

Objectively run through your stories of success to discover what hidden expectations you unknowingly have, which are in turn stopping you from getting what you want. I even have a guided template to walk you through just this problem in the *Success Rebel Go Guide* available at http://SuccessRebelBook.com

Believe.

Your intentions create your ability to influence.

Become.

Proactive in what you feed your mind. From the books you read to the movies and television you watch—everyone and everything has motive and intention. If you aren't clear about theirs—you may end up being consumed by it.

Connect.

Choose to rewrite your story, your patterns, and your expectations. You control your own narrative—no matter what The OTHERS say.

Chapter 16

THE STRUGGLE FOR SUCCESS MYTH

MAY YOU BE SO BLIND AS TO ONLY KNOW AND FOLLOW YOUR OWN HEART.

Question: If success is so natural and we are so smart, why do we struggle with living, being, and fully becoming the successes we dream of?

Answer: Because the success we think of isn't what we really dream of.

We all have dreams. Some are rooted from our heart, but many are planted by others. Sometimes these implanted dreams are innocent, sometimes they are not.

Your grandmother, for example, who wanted you to be a doctor. Since you were a little child she encouraged you and spoke about how amazing a future doctor you would be. Not your grandmother? Sometimes, dreams are implanted by modern social stories, movies and tv...one scene captures your mind of how you wish your life would be.

You think on and work towards these dreams. But these dreams do not root in you or your SOULFIRE. They first root in the imaginations of others. Therefore, these dreams in the end, will never fully fulfill you because it was never fully from within you.

WE MUST NEVER CONFUSE THE ACCEPTANCE OF OTHERS' SOULFIRES FOR ACCEPTANCE OF OURSELVES OR OUR SOULFIRE.

Though taking on the family business that has been around for over a hundred years or making your grandpa's wish of having a lawyer in the family may sound noble, nothing is noble when you fail to live up to your true purpose.

YOUR PURPOSE IS TO INSPIRE OTHERS BY BEING YOURSELF.

THE FALSEHOOD OF COMPETITION.

As human beings we need to see what is possible in others for us to know on many levels what is possible in ourselves.

The problem is that The OTHERS and surrounding social stories don't tell us "Imagine what you can do." They tell us "You need to be like them," "They are going to take your spot," "They are your competition."

THE OTHERS MISCONSTRUE SOMEONE ELSE'S DIVINE DREAM AND MAKES IT INTO A COMPETITION BETWEEN YOU AND THEM.

Let's be honest, it is a competition neither of you will win. They won't win because as soon as The OTHERS point out that you are now out to get them, beat them, conquer them, and take their spot—their mental, emotional, and spiritual energy is fractured not focused; likewise, yours as well.

A perfect example of that has been playing out in the United States political arena for the last five years. Love or don't love, President Trump, how he has been treated is a perfect example of how The OTHERS try to get you off of your Success Rebel path. How extreme, vicious, and draining their approach remains. To disrupt. To undermine.

The way President Trump has responded, though not always graceful, is how many Success Rebels come across when they refuse to bow down to the motives of The OTHERS. By design, Success Rebels are set up to be portrayed as irrational, not friendly, loners, selfish and self-absorbed.

And we can all agree that it has been an awfully lot of wasted time, resources, and energy simply because President Trump knows the truth about The OTHERS. He confirms the truth that you won't win if it isn't your dream.

FRACTURED FOCUS LESSENS ALL OF IMPACT AND INFLUENCE—AKA NOT FULLY LIVING THEIR LIFE OF NEW NOTORIETY.

LEARN.

You cannot let the falsehood of scarcity, competition, and mirroring others behavior invade your mind and heartscapes.

DO.

Audit how you spend your everyday life. Much time, resources, and energy can be wasted simply because you are fulfilling the expectations of others.

BELIEVE.

You are not in competition with anyone or thing on this side of Heaven. You are solely in partnership with the Divine.

BECOME.

Recognize that struggle means that you are out of alignment with your DIVINE PARTNERSHIP or SOULFIRE.

CONNECT.

Many of you have grown up with the mindset that "Success is hard" and "Money doesn't grow on trees." Find a community of new people with whom you hang out in person or online; watch that what you read and what you watch doesn't hold or promote old beliefs.

3

DECIDE IF YOU ARE WITH THE OTHERS OR ARE YOU AN OUTCAST

Chapter 17

WHY LIFE AND LOVE DON'T GO HAND IN HAND

MAY YOU ALWAYS KNOW FROM THE DEPTHS OF YOUR CORE THAT YOU ARE UNCONDITIONALLY LOVED AND WANTED.

One of the biggest lies that The OTHERS have gotten us to believe is that life and love go hand in hand. That if we choose to go after what they define as life, love will follow.

Meaning that if you go after an expensive education that it will create a good life for you. And in turn you will love your career and the life this education helps to create. You will get the love partner you have always desired and in turn the family, kids, and pups you have always wanted.

Or...if you pursue the relationships that make logical sense, commit to those that follow the path to a good life...that together you both will have a good life and in turn love your life.

Or...if you procreate smartly, wait until you are financially affluent, have the boy and the girl, raise them on the all organic, multi-language, soccer living path you will have a good life and in turn love it.

"SMART" MOVES DON'T ALWAYS EQUAL SUCCESSFUL ONES.

How many people do you know who have expensive degrees and hate their careers? Or have the expensive degree and the debt that comes with it, but work in a completely unrelated field simply because that is where they found work? Is that success? Is that love? Is that the life they dreamed of?

How about all those smart relationships that should have worked out? The marriages that looked good on paper. The business partnerships with the complementary skills sets that should have worked out beautifully to create the perfect business.

And do we even need to get into the facade of a story of what it is like to be a parent?

THE TRUTH IS: YOU DON'T FIND LIFE FIRST THEN
FIND LOVE. YOU HAVE TO HAVE LOVE FIRST
AND THEN THE LIFE YOU WANT WILL FOLLOW.

CHOOSE LOVE.

But love is messy. Love isn't logical. Love doesn't
follow a straight line. Love isn't controlling or
manipulative. So, The OTHERS don't want you to
know the power love holds for you. The restorative,
transformative, and soul healing qualities love has.

The way we each love is as different as our DNA and
our Divine gifts.

THE HEALING NATURE OF YOUR LOVE IS
UNIQUELY DESIGNED TO SOOTHE THE RAW
WOUNDS OF ANOTHER SOUL.

Your love is uniquely designed to look, feel, and
transform the souls your SOULFIRE is designed to
touch.

Yes, love is rooted from the Divine.

WHEN YOU FOCUS ON LOVE YOU FOCUS ON
TRANSFORMATION.

When you focus on love you focus on what makes you unique—your SOULFIRE.

When you choose the things you love, the people you love, the ways you uniquely love and allow the transformations your love creates—it washes over the world around you in whatever manner it chooses. That is when the life of success, enjoyment, fulfillment, influence, affluence, happiness, peace, favor, and NEW NOTORIETY will be there for you.

LEARN.

If you don't love it. You will never be truly successful at it.

DO.

Stop focusing on your "to do" list of success and focus on what sets your heart on fire.

BELIEVE.

Believe that your heart won't ever lead you astray.

BECOME.

Passionate about your passions. Stop wasting time on tasks, time suckers, and other wastes when you could be lighting your passions up every day.

CONNECT.

Engage with people who have similar passions and see the world your way.

Chapter 18

GET YOUR HEART ON STRAIGHT FIRST

WITHOUT LOVING YOURSELF FIRST, NOTHING ELSE CAN SUCCEED.

For the most part we live in a society of compromise.
We have no problem compromising our beliefs, values, standards, or vision to keep or gain the relationship, status, income, influence, or job we think we seek.

We like to think of ourselves as morally astute and uncompromising with our beliefs. The truth is if you want something bad enough, you will justify your way into anything.

And that is exactly how The OTHERS trap you. One single, slow justification at a time.

EXCUSE: Well, I can't 'keep the cat I have had for the last eight years because I am just too busy now that I got the promotion at work. Really? Is it really the promotion or the man you want to keep in your life who doesn't like your cat?

EXCUSE Well, I can't eat healthy because I don't have time to shop or meal prep every week. And we all know those box meal services are just overpriced. Really? Have you run the numbers, done research, and looked for a solution? Or were you just looking for an answer to justify what you really wanted all along—which was to feel good about keeping your unhealthy dietary habits.

The truth is many people want to know how to connect with their SOULFIRE simply because they think they want the payoff that being in partnership with the Divine can provide. They seek the solution to the desired outcome they want—not the solution for solution's sake. Meaning you would accept any solution that anyone says will get you the end result you seek.

The OTHERS know this. It hints why the self-help, health, and business development markets are so large. On average these markets combined gross well over 394 billion dollars a year. With professional/ business development making more than the self-help and health markets combined.

WE ALL KNOW THAT SUCH MASS INFORMATION DOESN'T REALLY WORK BECAUSE IF IT DID WE WOULD ALL BE UBER SUCCESSFUL, WEALTHY, AFFLUENT, INFLUENTIAL, HAPPY, AND HAVE A PACK OF UNICORNS RUNNING FREE IN OUR BACKYARDS.

Before you dive into the practical logistics of connecting, growing, developing, and truly walking out— for the partnership you desire with your unique SOULFIRE on a daily basis—a few mental and emotional switches must be flipped.

On some level these switches are really mental and emotional strongholds created through social stories and unrealistic expectations The OTHERS have put in place for you not to pursue your DIVINE PARTNERSHIP and in turn live a life of NEW NOTORIETY on a consistent basis.

STRONGHOLD 1: OUTCOME FOCUSED ONLY.

We don't like to admit it, but many of us simply do what we do for the payoff we are told we will receive.

Go to work and get paid.

Be grateful and get happy.

Engage with a person and have a beneficial relationship.

Give away your product or service and get a customer out of obligation.

OUR ACTIONS ARE MOTIVATED PURELY BY WHAT WE GET.

Our current society reeks of this mindset. And yet we live in a day and age where we are the unhappiest, feel the most disjointed, and though financially successful as a whole we continue to live with the "What about me?" mentality.

The reason for all this unhappiness is because motive matters. That's why doing little more than viewing and connecting with your SOULFIRE as a means to the esthetic life you want won't work.

STRONGHOLD 2: EXPECTATIONS OF THE EXPERIENCE.

Have you ever brought a child to a really nice restaurant?

One where the food, service and environment are on point? Where you know they will create a magical experience that your child will hold with them for the rest of their lives?

Besides being a great time in the moment you know that this will be an amazing learning experience for your child where they can see how to behave, act, dress, and speak in a manner that will come in handy as they navigate various life situations.

You plan this amazing experience. Make the reservation. Set up how magical of a night this will be. You pull out all of the stops to make the evening special. You put on nice clothes, clean up the car, make sure there are menu options the little one will like. Everything is set.

You have explained to your child how much fun this evening will be. The child has bought into the idea that this is going to be a positive, happy experience. But when the moment comes and your child is sitting across from you, their hamburger is "icky" because it isn't like how their favorite fast food chain does it.

And no matter what explanation you give, there is no appeasing your child. There is no saving the experience because though you prepared them for what is to come, this five-star meal isn't what they were expecting. In the end they want what they have always known, even though it isn't better. Even though it doesn't get them the goals, lifestyle, or experience they say they want.

Your kiddo leaves with the lesson that five-star meals are bad and "icky" all because their expectation of the experience was off.

This is how many of us are when it comes to going after what we say we want. We say we want to live a life of NEW NOTORIETY, to be influential in our industries and relationships, to be financially stable, affluent, and successful. But for any of that to happen we have to stand out. We have to go against the majority. We have to risk being rejected, judged, criticized, and shunned not by the unknown stranger, but by people we love, respect, and want to have a relationship with.

Though we have all heard such a thing, you don't know what that really means or will feel like to you until you are in the fancy restaurant and every ounce of your being can't take the experience because it is simply not what you have known.

STRONGHOLD 3: THE TECHNICALITY OF TIME.

Time is an illusion on many levels. From feeling the internal pressure that there is not enough time...to the idea that nothing has a sense of urgency...to certain tasks, which can only happen on certain days of the week or at certain hours of the day.

Who says that a true workday is from 9 to 5? Who says that Saturday and Sunday are the days we aren't supposed to be working? Who says that getting up at 3AM to work is crazy?

Time is just a constraint that we created. It is a pure illusion like most of the other social stories we hear from The OTHERS. We use time to help organize events in our mind, but the truth is—the passage of time or when things happen has nothing to do with time.

The limitations on time are arbitrary.

TIME IS A TOOL THAT SOCIETY AND THE OTHERS HAVE USED FOR YEARS TO CONTROL, MINIMIZE, AND SQUASH THE DIVINE DREAMS AND TRUE WORK OF THE MASSES.

Because when time is limited so is what, how, when, and with whom you can create and partner with.

The OTHERS also know that if they can limit when and where you feel like you can connect with your SOULFIRE, all they have to do is get you so busy with parental, marital, and life roles that years pass before you even pause to recognize that you have taken no action. Then guilt takes over and bingo-bango, The OTHERS have you just where they want you.

Pause for a moment and realize that time restrictions truly are man-made. Granted, we all have certain unmovable logistics in our lives, such as when our child needs to be picked up from school, but all the rest is truly up to us.

You don't have to believe the lies that after 8pm is Netflix time every night. Or that you can only do your errands on the weekend. Or only find God in the church building on Sunday morning.

THE TRUTH IS THAT YOU CONTROL YOUR TIME. YOU CONTROL THE WHEN AND THE HOW. WHEN YOU RECOGNIZE SUCH A MASSIVE TRUTH AND HOW POWERFUL IT IS, YOUR WORLDS CHANGE. LIVES CHANGE, AND YOUR

ABILITY TO TRULY TAP INTO THE POWER THAT
IS YOUR SOULFIRE IS UNLEASHED WITH WILD
ABANDONMENT.

STRONGHOLD 4: THE ILLUSION OF INSTANT.

We all know that we live in a society of instant.
From our food, to communication, to how fast an
online order should arrive. And though we know
that not everything is instant logically, this cultural
shift—from carefully curated and cared for to flying
out the door—has impacted us more than we realize.

We have less sex and are more stressed. We deal
with more depression and anxiety. Overall, we are
less happy and less optimistic. And even though the
economy increases equally to our use of technology
and the general speed of life, more money doesn't
make us feel more fulfilled.

HUMAN BEINGS ARE NOT BUILT TO BE SUPERSONIC SOLO.

We aren't meant to live at breakneck speeds
without, well...breaking our proverbial neck at some
point. While this seems more like a physical and
mental health related issue, the truth is: it is yet
another rooted lie from The OTHERS. This lie is not
designed to get you to think, live, or create the

DIVINE PARTNERSHIP and individuality that you are created to be.

It is an animal instinct to get accustomed to our surroundings. Noises, habits, speed—we get use to and in turn immune to our environments. Transfer horses from a quiet rural field that they have known their entire lives to a field that backs a busy highway and the horses will freak out. Same holds true in the reverse. If you go from living in a fast-paced environment to someplace where progress feels slow, accomplishments take a while to develop, and you aren't surrounded with noise, success, or people—and you will freak out too.

The OTHERS know this. They know that the majority of life is an instant one. From how fast you can travel, eat, power nap, buy a car or any other task of life—it is these tasks that can be instant, anything that is anything slower than instant will be too long.

Because instant makes us happy, at least for the short term. The emotional side of our brains can't imagine the future, so they want it NOW.

When we try to break ranks from The OTHERS, when we try to follow the yearnings of our souls, The OTHERS know that if we make it past their social story mind games, that eventually we ourselves are most likely to lose faith (or interest) and give up because the Divine isn't always instant.

The interesting thing is that the Divine is the only thing that can and really does do instant. Living your SOULFIRE is as much you as it is Him. It is a partnership after all. Like with all good partnerships, sometimes one partner is waiting for the other to catch up. That's us.

The slowness we experience is self-induced because if we are given our heart's desires right away, if we were given a life of NEW NOTORIETY instantly, we would never be committed to the root of the partnership. All of our ego needs would be met, and we wouldn't be committed to the core of our purpose—to serve others. We would only be focused on ourselves.

STRONGHOLD 5: IMPORTANCE OF SELF.

CONFUSION AND MISINTERPRETATION ARE THE TWO GREATEST TACTICS THAT THE OTHERS USE TO STOP US FROM FULLY CONNECTING AND LIVING OUR SOULFIRE AND IN TURN ENJOYING THE BLESSINGS THAT COME FROM A LIFE OF NEW NOTORIETY.

One of the biggest points of confusion is with the idea of self.

In one corner you have the ideology that self is bad. That you must be last, act like, and be a servant. Because ego, pride, and a host of other ungodly virtues will ensue and eventually kill your soul.

And in the other corner, you have the modern-day social stories that say" You Matter." Every ounce of you matters. Every thought, action, reaction, feeling, idea—it's all brilliant, important, and should be valued and heard.

When we step back and look at these two ideologies with any ounce of honest perspective we realize the craziness that they both are. The first one is a misquote from the Bible.

The scripture "Do you want to stand out? Then step down. Be a servant. If you puff yourself up, you'll get the wind knocked out of you. But if you're content to simply be yourself, your life will count for plenty."

~ Matthew 23:11-12 The Message (MSG)

This scripture is talking about the heart of a servant not the mindset of one. Many people clearly don't remember being a teenager because every idea, thought, and belief that goes through anyone's mind doesn't need to be shared for so many reasons.

No matter how you should happen to lean on the idea of self, I can guarantee you aren't fulfilling your true DIVINE PARTNERSHIP because you have a distorted view of you. And just like the illusion of instant—our ideas of self-stop us before we ever achieve.

TAPPING INTO YOUR SOULFIRE IS A TRUE PARTNERSHIP.

Yet, true partnership is an idea we have a hard time understanding because we don't see many. Nothing like the reality TV marriages you see portrayed on any show from the *Real Housewives* to *90-Day Fiancé.*

A true partnership is about respect for each other, having a clearly defined vision or purpose, having an agreed upon outcome when it comes to success, lifestyle, etc., knowing each other's roles and responsibilities, and doing them no matter what.

Far too often we want the outcome and we have passion around the purpose. It's the rest of the partnership pieces we aren't fond of because it requires us to overcome our own negative mindset, reevaluate our ego, and do things that— and when— we really don't want to do sometimes.

A successful partnership in life or in conjunction with living your SOULFIRE is a balance of:

> Unapologetically knowing your worth and value as well as that of your partners
>
> The goals you collectively have; and
>
> The commitment to your agreed upon vision and outcomes outranks any personal moments of self-doubt.

STRONGHOLD 6: THE SOLO VS. TEAM CONUNDRUM.

The idea of duality is one only found on this side of Heaven. The OTHERS know that if all else fails, duality will stop people in their tracks because no side wins.

Plus, for all of the highly logical and intelligent people out there, duality short-circuits the brain...because both arguments have opposing flaws in their beliefs and in turn in their rebuttals. This type of mindset, therefore, stops most people from realizing the flawed and manipulated logic in the first place. They and their brains are caught in a mental loop of chaos they can't escape.

Case in point, the idea of teamwork yet the praising of solo success.

Many of us were raised with teams. Teams in sports. Teams in schools. We were taught that no one wins unless the group wins.

Our love affair with teams goes back to our primal beginnings as hunters and gatherers. The community—aka the team—must "win" to survive. And though many of us have not experienced life in such a collective community our cells certainly have.

The theory of cellular memories states that memories and personality traits are stored not only in the brain but in the cells and organs. Beyond our own memories,
The Emory University Medical School discovered "transgenerational epigenetic inheritance," which

means cellular memory can be passed down from generation to generation.

And the Bible even talks about generational cellular memories,

"Keeping steadfast love for thousands, forgiving iniquity and transgression and sin, but who will by no means clear the guilty, visiting the iniquity of the fathers on the children and the children's' children, to the third and the fourth generation."

~ Exodus 34:7 ESV

Yet we enter society and though the idea of teams is promoted, the truth we are actually presented with is that success is best solo. Promotions happen solo. One company wins the bid, one lead on the project, one "overnight" success. We are obsessed with the idea of one.

The idea of one has its own social connotations. Being #1, being the best, no competition, total leader, revolutionary, transformational. And of course, when we look at numerology we see the subconscious beliefs in:

- Being connected to the Creator.
- A doer and power force.
- Strong, determined, unwavering with specific goals in mind.
- Growth and transformation.
- In alignment with nature and biology.

- and straightforward.

- Simple A ruthless warrior.

So, who wouldn't be #1? Even if it meant being solo.

Like with our duality. If you remember the opening scene of the film Star Trek II—we have a Kobayashi Maru situation here—aka a no-win scenario.

NO MATTER IF YOU MAKE IT SOLO OR WITH A TEAM YOU ARE SET UP TO BELIEVE THAT YOU WERE SUPPOSED TO HAVE "MADE IT" THE OTHER WAY.

This no-win battle doesn't just happen in your head. The people around you will point out the dichotomy as well. Have this happen over and over again on your journey to success and even the strongest minds will begin to cave.

THAT'S WHY IT IS SO KEY TO HAVE AN ANCIENT ROMAN AND GREEK PERSPECTIVE, IN WHICH WE PARTNER WITH THE DIVINE SPIRIT.

It is the only mindset that blends the idea of team—aka—the partnership between you and the Divine—and the art of solo because the outside world will only see you.

STRONGHOLD 7: THE PARADOX OF BEING KNOWN.

If you haven't figured it out by now, mind games are the "go to" game of The OTHERS. They know if they can confuse you they can stop you. Even when it comes to success.

Yes, in spite of all of the social stories out there around success —YOU MUST HAVE SUCCESS—we also clearly see that success comes with a cost.

It comes with getting kicked out of our current tribe. It comes with haters and back stabbers. It comes with loss, risk, and people looking to tear you down. For as much potential growth and love there could be, the story of the one-hit wonder has scared us more than the potential for greatness has inspired us.

But if we paused for a moment and recognized what those stories really were, the truth would appear: they are simply stories.

Those stories were written by someone, somewhere else for their good and of the good of The OTHERS. When you can get to the real perspective then you can recognize that you, too are the same. They are a story writer —there is a story writer inside of you; you are equally yoked. Actually, you are better at this because studies show that we believe the sound of our own voice more than another person's.

STOP LETTING THE OTHERS USE THE POWER OF YOUR OWN VOICE TO THEIR ADVANTAGE.

Rewrite the story of success for you. Tap into your SOULFIRE and ask your Divine partner what it is that you are truly creating. Write your story and see the successes unfold.

LEARN.
Your success or failure begins in your mind.

DO.
Start daydreaming intentionally to overcome the strongholds that have been embedded in you and to propel your SOULFIRE forward.

BELIEVE.
Your mind is more powerful than you know.

BECOME.
Begin to act, speak, dress, behave, think, and react as the person you see in your mind's eye. Choosing such actions consciously will propel your success into the life of NEW NOTORIETY.

CONNECT.
Consciously investigate the strongholds that may be holding you back and connect with like-minded people who speak the truth about their strongholds and how they positively move forward.

Chapter 19

THE ULTIMATE HURT

MAY THE HURT THAT IS MEANT TO HARM YOU NEVER HIT YOUR HEART.

There comes a moment in life that seems relatively innocent at the time but ends up creating the ULTIMATE HURT. The hurt that THE OTHERS hope will turn you away from your SOULFIRE and living a life of NEW NOTORIETY.

For many of us, The OTHERS' design for this hurt to happen early on in life. This way you quickly abandon your Divine longing because you don't have the mental fortitude to realize what is happening. Or you simply don't have the mental strength to go against the social story or authority figure at play.

PEOPLE AND PAIN.

One of my earliest ULTIMATE HURTS happened when I was around 12 years old. One summer day, Lilly, my surrogate grandmother of sorts, took me out to the barn to take care of my horses, Can Do and Shogun. My parents were out of town for their summer vacation and the responsibilities of the horses and barn cats were on me.

We were heading to leave the barn one afternoon, when my grandfather pulled up with a trailer full of construction debris. Broken glass, rusty nails, you name it—it was in there. He informed me that he planned on dumping the rubble in the field with my horses and setting it on fire.

Well, even at 12 years old I knew that was a moronic idea. So, I refused. I stood in front of his truck and would not let him in. I simply refused. Lilly and I didn't head home that day until he was long gone.

Needless to say, when my parents got back, World War III was in full force at my house. I was told to apologize, asked who I thought I was, and included in a tirade of the social stories about respecting your elders. But I refused. I refused because I fervently believed I was entrusted with protecting lives and souls. Those horses, that barn, those cats— each was my responsibility to protect. And that is what I did!

This battle waged on for months. My father refused to defend me, but he also did not force me to make amends either—until my birthday.

When my birthday rolled around, this "war" was six months in. I had not thought of ever apologizing for it because I'd done nothing wrong. Period—end of story in my book. My grandfather said he wanted to give me a birthday gift, but the only way I could receive it was if I went and met him in his office.

My dad wanted me to go and my mom asked me to as well. I don't remember what was said specifically, but I do remember how I felt. I left feeling how I would assume a prostitute feels.

It wasn't that money was exchanged. It wasn't that I felt he got the upper hand. It wasn't that I felt that I sold out. It was that no one cared to acknowledge that I did the right thing—that my father didn't want to defend me. And that the only man at that time who did seem to care about me, my grandfather, didn't care an ounce about me because I wouldn't fall into line.

TEN THOUSAND LITTLE CUTS.

Innocent enough of a situation in the beginning, right?

Those are the kind of situations The OTHERS love because even if they are verbalized or seen—nothing seems all that horrible. We aren't talking about abuse or neglect.

146

WE ARE TALKING ABOUT ONE COMMENT, ONE LOOK, ONE INTERACTION, ONE SITUATION, ONE EXPERIENCE—EACH WITH THE POTENTIAL TRAJECTORY TO GET YOU OFF THE PATH TO YOUR DESTINY—NOT JUST YOUR LIFE, BUT YOUR DIVINE CALLING.

Because of the innocent nature, most likely the other party or parties involved will never remember the incident. That too is by design. Because years later you still remember that defining moment. Logically it shouldn't matter to you. You can see that with retrospective logic. But living the life you feel called to, living a life of NEW NOTORIETY isn't about logic. It is about being led. The OTHERS know this.

They know the Divine side and calling on your life. They know how a paper cut can hurt more than a true battle wound.

Because the ULTIMATE HURT is the ultimate because of its surprising and unexpected occurrence.

IT'S THE ULTIMATE HURT BECAUSE IT IS A SPIRITUAL TOOL BROUGHT INTO THE REALM OF HUMAN INTERACTION.

It is dynamically designed to create a seemingly insignificant wound that you move on from not knowing the infection and scar it is creating.

Do you have to know the moment your ULTIMATE HURT happened? No. But many of us do. Many of us think about those hurts as a passing thought or moment of melancholy.

OUR LOGICAL MINDS DISMISS IT AND OUR HEARTS ACHE BECAUSE OUR HEARTS HAVE A TRUER UNDERSTANDING OF OUR SOUL'S DESIRE THAN OUR MINDS EVER WILL.

LEARN.

Hurts happen in life, but it is how you heal that matters.

DO.

We all have pain. We all have hurts. Begin to actively reframe them so that you can break free of the holds The OTHERS have on you.

BELIEVE.

You are fully capable of overcoming every pain, every hurt that comes your way. And yes, I know that sucks when you are in the middle of all of it.

BECOME.

Pain happens on this side of Heaven. When we stay in the flow of our SOULFIRE and remain committed to our DIVINE PARTNERSHIP, the pain is more palatable.

CONNECT.

Talk and move on. Find a great therapist, friend, your cat, and talk it out. When you verbalize how you feel you are able to release not just the thoughts but the energetics of the experience as well.

Chapter 20

THE ULTIMATE TEST YOU MUST PASS TO LIVE A SUCCESSFUL LIFE

MAY EVERY OBSTACLE ACCELERATE YOUR SUCCESS.

Most people hear the word "test" and want to run. The word "test" is one of those words that creates a physical, emotional, and primal reaction for many of us. Depending upon whether you loved or didn't love school so much, your view of the written word is colored. Though many of us have been out of school for years, the truth is that the tests don't stop coming.

Because of our schooling, we expect the tests to come with notice, in a logical order and with spacing. Yet that isn't how life rolls. Sometimes these tests are small—such as how you are going to react to a situation, are you going to stress eat a pint of ice cream before bed, or are you going to make another excuse about why you don't have the relationship you really want?

There comes a moment when the whopper of all whoppers of a test heads your way. This is the one test you must pass if you want to achieve your dreams, live a life of NEW NOTORIETY, and thrive in your DIVINE PARTNERSHIP on all levels. Basically, if you truly want to succeed.

PUSH OR PAUSE TEST.

I like to call these whoppers, the Push or Pause (P/P) tests. I know, not the sexiest name, but it is ridiculously accurate because it makes you choose. Are you going to push or are you going to pause?

Everyone's P/P test looks different. I know this because after working with entrepreneurs and business founders for over two decades, I have never seen two P/Ps ever appear the same. There are some common threads like timing and triggers, but the HOW is always unique because it is built from your deepest subconscious fears.

MY FIRST CAREER RELATED P/P HAPPENED WHEN I WAS 28 YEARS OLD.

Almost ten years into my career and I was finally figuring things out. My message, my audience, my passion for my work both in the big picture and every day.

Doors and opportunities were opening. National press, television, speaking opportunities and professional collaborations that you dream of. With every opportunity it didn't just create exposure for my work, it created exposure for me. As in ME—on stage, TV, pictures—the works.

Now that may not seem like such a big deal in the Instagram, selfie obsessed society we live in today. But back then it wasn't common. Also, back then I looked very different than I do today because I was still dealing on a daily basis with the physical ramifications of the toxic mold exposure I had six years prior.

Besides physically just not feeling well, I didn't look well either. My weight would fluctuate from a size 14 maternity to a size 22 maternity within a matter of days. And no, I have never been pregnant. Because my body couldn't regulate itself concerning temperatures, food, or the environment I was in. My body was always overreacting, and those around me never knew what they were going to get; neither did I!

Yet I had these opportunities that required me to stop hiding and get out there. But would anyone listen to what a severely overweight woman had to say? Would I do my brand more harm than good?

Would I build positive relationships with the audience, TV producers, and contributors or would they think that I was "not" TV or national material?

I had to decide whether I was going to push through how I physically felt. Push through my mindset about no longer being the size zero like I was before the toxic mold exposure. Push through the mental stress of what The OTHERS were going to say. Or was I going to pause until my health and my appearance were more socially acceptable?

THE SECOND TEST HAPPENED A LITTLE OVER TEN YEARS INTO MY MARRIAGE.

For me marriage truly was "till death do us part." Call it my Scorpio ways, but I am a ride or die type of loyalist when I make a commitment. And though my husband and I never were truly happy in our marriage, I was going to honor the commitment first and figure out the logistics of life later.

Well, my husband at the time was also my business partner. We had closed his medical practice because it wasn't his love and he joined my work. We traveled and did everything together. He handled the day to day activities so I could deal with the clients, media, book writing, and brand growth.

For me this was great because even though I wasn't madly, passionately in love with him or him with me— everything I did was for our family. I worked for our family. Put in all-nighters for our family. Built out new brands for future income streams so our cash flow wasn't tied to my time or ability to produce. I was building a brand legacy that would be a nest egg for him if I was here or not. Call it my version of life insurance.

But one day, when things were finally looking like we were going to make a turn for the better, my husband decided he wanted to leave the marriage, the business—and my life—for good.

Out of the blue on many levels, and honestly the smartest move in the long term, the shock of being alone, having no one else to shoulder the responsibilities big and small, and losing the person who I thought had my back for the rest of my life, was devastating. It was the first time in my career that I questioned if I was in the right line of work.

I had to decide if I was going to push forward with my career. Push forward saying "yes" to clients and building these brands even though I no longer had a family. Would I push through when it came to life, commitments, and never failing the clients no matter how I physically felt? Or was I going to pause, give up on everything I had worked for and play it safe with a 9-5 job?

THE THIRD TEST HAPPENED TWO YEARS INTO THE LAUNCH OF MY PRODUCTION AND NETWORK COMPANIES.

I never consciously wanted to open up a production company or digital television network, but I saw the need for such platforms for my clients and myself. I knew such ventures would take time to create and build up. So as with everything in my career, why not just start?

Two years into creating what is now an
international award-winning show for
entrepreneurs and building my version of HGTV for
entrepreneurs, shit was going down behind the
scenes. My predominantly male crew was suffering
from testosterone terrors.

It didn't matter how many "come to Jesus" talks we
had, meetings about expectations, meetings about
making sure that their personal life goals were met.
you name the leadership style method or HR people
handling style, I tried it. But in spite of all of that
effort, I had a very unhappy crew who had no
problem lying, cheating, and stealing from me.

Now we aren't talking about paper clip worthy theft,
we are talking about big boy, big money, and big
intellectual property. Therefore, with both the
production and network companies still largely self-
funded by *moi*, such anarchy logically would have
taken its toll.

I had to decide if I was going to push through
financially and find a way to recoup my losses. Push
through mentally in spite of their disregard for
honoring their contractual relationship and work
scope agreements. Push through to keep striving for
what I knew these projects were capable of even
though it put me in a financial situation that was
beyond idiotic on paper. Or was I going to pause
because it was not safe for me to keep going?

ARE YOU GOING TO PUSH OR PAUSE?

At no point in any of those moments where I had to decide to push or pause did I have a clear unmistakable understanding about what to do. And at every single instance, the logical, rational, smart, socially acceptable decision to make was to pause. Yet I knew for me, that to pause was to die.

I knew in my heart of hearts, which for me is in the area of the heart chakra, that I had to push. Just like there comes a moment where a woman in labor knows she has to push; I knew that I had to push. And just like a woman in active labor, it wasn't easy, but there was an unexplainable peace when I made the choice and took action.

After every push, breakthrough happened.

After my first push, I became a three-time bestselling author.

After my second push, my branding career and exposure went to truly luxury levels.

And after my most recent push, the team I always dreamed of, corporate partners, collaborators, and audience showed up.

The P/P tests never come at the most opportune times. They typically come when you are already giving your all. You are thinking about your breakthrough, that life of NEW NOTORIETY, and success should be right around the corner. On many levels it is, but you have to pass the test first.

P/Ps show you your greatest fears. I have seen clients have ex—boyfriends appear. Some people get unexplainably sick...while others struggle with a great personal loss. Your P/Ps will bring up your deepest darkest fears. This is one reason why I have never seen two P/Ps manifest the same way. My P/Ps brought up my subconscious fears of men, money, and making a difference.

Like the NBC public service announcement slogan said every Saturday morning, "Knowledge is power." By simply knowing about the Push or Pause tests you will be equipped to understand and pass the next one you face.

KNOW THAT THOUGH THIS TEST WILL FEEL MISERABLE IN THE MOMENT, JUST AROUND THE CORNER THE SUCCESS AND LIFE OF NEW NOTORIETY AWAITS YOU.

LEARN.

You are in total control about how you react.

DO.

When situations come, ask your Divine Partner, "Do I push or pull?"

BELIEVE.

Choosing the solution that works best for you, no matter how illogical it looks, is still the right choice for you.

BECOME.

Tune your awareness into the bigger situation at hand. Stop being reactionary in the moment and look at the bigger landscape. Consider the bigger story at play. Become the person who takes unapologetic decisive action about when to push and when to pause.

CONNECT.

Practice makes perfect, but let's be honest, you really don't want to have to practice this all that much. Find a community of like-minded people who openly model such behavior so that you can learn from others—and not just your experiences.

Chapter 21

YOUR DREAMS HAVE IT

MAY THE DREAMS OF YOUR BIRTH ALWAYS LIGHT UP YOUR SOUL.

Growing up we all have dreams. For many of us though, somewhere along the way we buy into the lie that our dreams are unrealistic fairy tales that just waste our time, resources, and energy. Instead, we pursue something that could never be a reality. This dream-crushing message is normally delivered by a trusted loved one. Therefore, we believe that pursuing our dreams will only lead to heartache and financial headaches.

YET WE ARE BORN WITH DREAMS.

Many religions—from Hinduism to Christianity—talk about having a purpose for our life. And though research shows children do not dream until around the age of seven or eight, we have all heard those stories of four-year-old children who talk about past lives, seeing angels, and have a knowledge that far surpasses their age.

It isn't just natural; it is built into our DNA. As we have previously discussed, the cells in our body, not just in our brain, store memories from past experiences in our life as well as those of our ancestors.

Your original, uninfluenced dreams are as unique as you are. No two dreams are exactly the same. The why, how, when, where, and intentionality behind each desire of your heart is unique to you. In that reality alone, most people underestimate the power their dreams have.

Many of us equate dreams with wishes and fairy tales. We write off the message our dreams show us. They are actually the missing piece that most of us pray for—they are the signs, the next steps, and the reason why you are here on this side of Heaven.

Your dreams truly are the road markers on your life's journey. They give you insight into who you are, what you are about, who and how you will influence, and what your successful life—your life of NEW NOTORIETY will look like. They reveal the depth of your SOULFIRE and the purpose of your DIVINE PARTNERSHIP. All the while, these dreams are the flashing warning sign of what opportunities to say "yes" to and which ones will only get you off track.

YOUR DREAMS TRULY ARE THE ROAD MARKERS ON YOUR LIFE'S JOURNEY.

Because our dreams mean so much to us, it is only instinctual to share them with others, search for feedback and gain confirmation that "yes" you are not insane. We look for signs that say "yes, you should totally follow your dreams." Unfortunately, in that act The OTHERS are allowed to play, pervert, and crush the potential right out of you.

Of course, no one can understand your dreams fully, see the depth of the influence and transformation of life that you can create because no one else has your vision, destiny, or heart. They aren't you and their gifting doesn't lie where yours does.

DREAMS ARE BEST BIRTHED IN THE DEPTHS OF YOUR HEART.

So, what are your unbiased dreams telling you?

First we have to get to your unbiased dreams. What people normally rattle off as their dreams aren't their dreams at all. They are the socially acceptable list of "dreams" that society allows for but aren't really yours. You will never truly go after them because they aren't worth the social risk to your personal well-being.

That is the number one check to know if what you say is your dream—really is your dream.

WOULD YOU DO ANYTHING TO SEE YOUR DREAM BE A REALITY?

Working with entrepreneurs for over 20 years, I have heard a lot of dreams and a lot of people saying, "Yes, I'll do anything for it!" But 9 times out of 10 when the workload gets tough, the money gets tight, or when they have to step outside of their comfort zone—the dream is no longer wanted. Therefore, it wasn't really their dream, or your dream, in the first place.

Yes, deep soul searching and guided SOULFIRE work can help remove some of the dreams of others before you invest too much of yourself into a goal. But many times, only time will tell when you are unwilling or unable to do the personal mental, emotional, and spiritual work needed to get clear on you and your goals.

Once you begin to crack the influence of the social stories and The OTHERS, your dreams will emerge. Write them down and share them with nobody. Don't judge them, edit them, or refine them.

RAW DREAMS ARE BEAUTIFUL BECAUSE IN THAT RAW FORM YOU WILL SEE THE COMMONALITIES OF YOUR ROAD MARKERS.

Because it is hard to talk about someone else's dreams and what they really mean to you, let me

share with you about mine. When you take a
retrospective look at everything that has ever
excited me, made me genuinely happy and that I was
intuitively good at—there were always two elements
that appeared.

One, I have always liked being above the standard in
the way things are presented. I have always been
fascinated by presentation, environments, spaces,
how objects and colors interact and move the
energy, and how each create emotions. I have always
felt that everything functional should be esthetically
beautiful and vice versa.

So yes, I always went the extra mile on my class
projects. In fourth grade it was no skimpy castle my
Dad and I built for the history fair. It was beautiful.
And I am pretty sure it is highly unusual for a kid to
constantly be moving the furniture around in her
bedroom, but I did.

The second thing about everything I do relates to
creating connections. Having people be able to
pause and breathe for a moment. To know that there
is respect, honor, and love for them and the
relationships we have. I guess these each hint to
why I always brought flowers to my teachers in
elementary school or made sure my mom brought
the yummy snacks for the class. I wasn't trying to
kiss up to the teacher or make friends. To me all
these people had so much sadness and anger, that
showing a bit of love was the only way to soothe it.

It is clearly evident that all my dreams deal with
quality and visual excellence. Therefore, beauty is
part of the SOULFIRE and DIVINE PARTNERSHIP path.
Because all of my dreams are about showing, giving,

or creating the experience for love to be felt—then clearly love is part of my SOULFIRE and my way to success.

And if all of this sounds overwhelming, don't worry, in the *Success Rebel Go Guide* I have created for you, I walk you through how to discern the roots of your dreams and the unique foundation for your SOULFIRE and success. You can grab your complimentary digital copy of the *Success Rebel Go Guide* at: http://successrebelbook.com.

DON'T JUDGE THE "HOW." IT IS THE "WHY" THAT HAS THAT SOUL CONNECTION AND SUCCESS DRIVEN POWER IN IT FOR YOU.

Once you understand what roots your road markers and dreams, you know what will bring you the ultimate success spiritually, emotionally, physically, financially, mentally, and within your relationships. These road markers now can be used as a litmus test to every opportunity or idea that is presented to you. If it doesn't hold the core being of your "whys" it isn't for you and won't bring you influence or success.

LEARN.
The innocence of your youth can give you the biggest insights to the real you.

DO.
Audit your loves from your first memories and then move forward from your earliest loves to present day. When you understand the "why" that has innately driven you all these years, then you will understand the "why" to your SOULFIRE work.

BELIEVE.
Youthful innocence doesn't have to equate to ignorance. Innocence can equal Divine intelligence.

BECOME.
Be bold enough to follow the roots of your dreams and determined enough to develop them into experiences that make a difference.

CONNECT.
Shocker! Connection and community go hand in hand. Once you reconnect with your SOULFIRE—begin to take steps in exploring what that looks like and feels like today in your life. Share the emotions that come forth with a group of likeminded people who won't judge, comment, or give advice, but instead will hold the space for you to grow. That is what the Success Rebel Society is all about and that is exactly why I created it. I can only hold the space for so many, but together we can hold the space for the masses.

4

TRANSFORM YOUR BLACK SHEEP WAYS INTO SUCCESS REBEL GLORY

Chapter 22

WHY CHANGE IS OVERRATED

When you hear the word "change" what do you think of? Personal growth or the coins in your pocket?

When it comes to personal growth, the idea of change is buzzy. We all want change. Or is it just the "in" thing to say? All life is change, but isn't it ironic that no one wants the change?

Society teaches us that change is really the leftovers. We feel like Plan Bs in business, money, or success. Not the best, nor the first. We want to be the masters of our domains and creators of our fortunes.

This social dichotomy may not be consciously affecting you, but it is subconsciously sabotaging your efforts to grow, evolve, and change. And The OTHERS love it that way. The buzz keeps you spinning your wheels doing, but never getting anywhere. Yep, your life is the epitome of burning rubber.

I'll be honest with you, personal change isn't bullsh*t with regards to how The OTHERS sell it. The idea that anyone can become anything they want because they BELIEVE that they are is idiotic.

I CAN BELIEVE ALL THAT I WANT THAT I'M A CAT, BUT THAT WON'T MAKE ME ONE.

Allowing such fanciful delusions to become a reality may seem innocent at first, but it harms the subconscious mind and our ability to truly succeed in ways that as a society or race we haven't seen in our lifetimes.

THE WORST DAMAGE TO SUCH DELUSIONAL THINKING DOES IS THAT IT FOCUSES OUR EFFORTS AND ENERGIES ON SOMETHING THAT COULD NEVER BE VS. FOCUSING ON THE PERSONAL EVOLUTION THAT IS IN OUR POWER.

As human beings we have complex motives, personalities, and capabilities. Even with how much brain power we have use of during our lifetimes, most of us fail to fully use all aspects of our unique personality to our life's advantage.

Why is this?

CAPABILITY FOCUSED.

Many of us don't have a true understanding of what we are capable of. We view ourselves through the lens of The OTHERS. Even if we try to gain insights into ourselves through personality assessments and aptitude tests, these outlets don't give us a framework of what the possibilities could be, how for us to take action and in turn succeed.

Early on in my branding work, my luxury branding client base included C-suite execs and Wall Street middle management types. My clients were striking out on their own, but they were failing to understand the potential they had. They failed to understand the people they were trying to bring on board to their project. Yes, these very SMART people were FAILING people.

This, my friends is where and when NERI was born. Neuro Emotional Relationship Intelligence (NERI) is a twofold system I developed and have used, trained, and implemented for over twenty years.

NERI is twofold in the sense that the information can be viewed in two ways.

1. One—from a personal perspective of who you are, what you are capable of, what your fundamental triggers, motives, and wants out of life include for you to feel like you are a success.

2. Another—from an outward perspective, regarding what the people you meet and interact with, truly want from their lives.

NERI IS DESIGNED TO CREATE BETTER RELATIONSHIPS WITH YOURSELF AND OTHERS BY QUICKLY FINDING ORGANIC COMMON GROUND TO ENGAGE THE BIOLOGICAL TENDENCIES OF "KNOW, LIKE, TRUST" TO YOUR RELATIONSHIP'S ADVANTAGE

But let's focus on you for the moment. Because this book is designed to be all about you, your success, your possibilities, and your life.

- What if you knew that you could authentically come across more powerfully in situations where right now you feel like a little church mouse?

- What if you knew that by simply asking for contracts or work orders to be delivered in a checklist format you would minimize your stress and anxiety levels significantly?

- What if you knew how to show people your "softer" side without coming across as weak, vulnerable, or saying a word?

- What if you could understand someone else's expectations for a relationship before you ever met them?

- What if you could consciously choose how you show up in all aspects of your life allowing you to evolve into the best version of yourself and never once be inauthentic to who you are, your SOULFIRE, DIVINE PARTNERSHIP, or life of NEW NOTORIETY you want to lead?

That is exactly what NERI does.

SUCCESS AND BEING A SUCCESS REBEL ISN'T ABOUT CHANGING INTO SOMEONE ELSE. IT IS ABOUT EVOLVING INTO WHO YOU HAVE ALWAYS BEEN FULLY CAPABLE OF BEING.

Part of that evolution is owning the real, core you by owning the emotional experience.

EMOTIONS VS. FEELINGS.

The OTHERS have done a brilliant job to get and keep people being obsessed with their feelings. They act as if they have no control over how they feel. This lie is perfect for The OTHERS because it keeps you stuck, in a victim mentality, and a burden to the Success Rebels who are trying to break free.

THE BIOLOGICAL TRUTH IS THAT FEELINGS ARE A CHOICE.

You can't, I can't, no one can—make you feel something you don't choose.

That truth doesn't mean people can't use your psychology, your biology, your social stories, your subconscious mind and environments to set you up for a certain emotion to occur. This happens all the time in interior design, with movies, and music. Good artists, designers, actors, and directors know just how to move the energy to create the emotion. But you still have total control over how you feel.

This is how two people can watch the same Hallmark ad and respond differently. One cries like a baby and the other person has no idea why.

The OTHERS love to use your biology against you. And crying over an ad or not may seem innocent, but it is one of the most potentially damaging manipulations that can happen. Because it creates zero responsibility, no clear boundaries of the do's and don'ts, and has no resolution. Worst of all the who, what, why, and how can change instantly because shifting feelings is what people who don't have a purpose do.

My ex-husband was a doctor. And watching the patients in his practice was some of the best people watching around because you could tell who the Success Rebels were and who were brainwashed by THE OTHERS.

Every new patient would come in saying, "I want to get better." Over a few months the proof was in their results. Every patient, for the most part, would see some type of improvement, but there always came a tipping point where the patient either truly loved that they were getting better and excelled from there or they started to complain about getting better.

"Well, yes, "a" is better but "y" now hurts." Or, "Yes, I'm feeling better, but I still can't run a marathon." There was always a "but" to the patient's "better." Because they identified with their illness; they liked how it made them feel psychologically even if they didn't like how they felt physically. They liked how people treated them because they were sick.

WHAT DO YOU IDENTIFY AS?

When your identity—and in turn—your coveted relationships are tied to your feelings, you will never leave them no matter how harmful they are to you or the others you love. That is your human biology in action. The OTHERS know this and use it against you to stay stuck personally or through the relationships you keep.

Now such irrational feelings don't just happen when we are physically weak and don't feel good. I see them within my private luxury branding clients all the time. This even happens on the reality tv show I host, *Fix My Brand With Ali Craig*, which airs on Apple TV's Notoriety Network, which follows real brands from around the world as they go from fledgling to fierce competition.

To create such a show in a timely manner, the brands have to stay on a strict rebrand schedule. By week four in the process, most of the back-end work is done. Decisions have been made. Now it is time to start taking action.

This is also normally when these entrepreneurs freak the hell out.

THEY QUESTION EVERYTHING. THEY WANT TO RETHINK, REDO IT, AND REGRET EVEN SAYING "YES" TO BEING ON THE SHOW.

Why is that?

It is because of how these otherwise accomplished people identify as a certain type of business as owner. Often, they are not as successful as they say they want to be, so they hold onto certain feelings rather than deal with the uncertainty of all that could be possible.

What if they did live all their dreams?

What if they did earn 10x their income in one year?

What if they could make more money, be happier, and work less?

FEELINGS ARE FUNNY, BUT THEY ARE CHOICES.
CHOOSE WISELY.

LEARN.

The real you has far more depth than the current patterns, mindsets, and habits by which you live. When you understand your NERI profile, you empower yourself to choose different habits, mindsets, patterns, or different perspectives, which all are intuitively you.

Do.

Delve deep into the possibilities that you are. The NERI website (http://neri.io) has many free resources that will allow you to understand your unique NERI makeup. You owe it to yourself to role play in your mind how acting, being, thinking, and behaving differently than you are today—but still within your NERI profile—could change the outcome of the habitual cycles you find yourself in.

BELIEVE.

You are more than your habits.

BECOME.

Become a chooser. Choose how you show up. Choose the experiences you want to create for yourself and for others. Choose the emotions you want to feel. Choose vs. blindly following.

CONNECT.

People watching is one of the best ways to understand the NERI method in others and in yourself.

Find a great place where you can sit and watch interactions that have substance. Meaning—not just people walking quickly by on the street—a review, an assessment of the biological, nonverbal and style traits the core NERI profiles have, and then hypothesize on just who these people are.

This is actually one of my favorite things to do solo but is a training exercise I lead during many of the boutique events I run every year. You too, will find it amazing, just what you can discern from people's behavior when you understand the possibilities that lie within.

Chapter 23

WHY YOU MUST BE ABLE TO DEFINE SUCCESS ON YOUR OWN TERMS

MAY YOU NEVER FORGET YOU WERE UNIQUELY DESIGNED FOR THIS.

Success is built into our DNA. As we now know from science—just because a gene is in your DNA it doesn't mean that it is automatically activated. That innate desire to succeed, to matter, to change the world, your way isn't a guarantee.

We all know this when we pause and look around. Most people struggle and never live a life of success that matters to them.

The OTHERS know this, and this is one reason why their attack through suppression is so multi-faceted. From the mind games of self-doubt and worth, to the relationship pressures, social stories, and just the pure exhaustion of trying to get your basic core needs met. All of this is designed to suppress your DNA.

Yes, your 21,000 DNA genes and 3 million rungs of material on your DNA ladder aren't triggered to be "on" all the time.

Your cell's RNA—through a process called RNAI, helps to identify which DNA genes they need on—and when. Similar to a house's circuit breaker box, the RNA can turn on or off a specific gene's ability-just like you can turn off a room's electricity by flipping a breaker's switch. But just as with your DNA, switched on or off, the "possibility" is still there.

YOU CAN HAVE ALL THAT YOU DESIRE.

But the desire and possibilities are still inside of you. So, no matter how far away, small, or impossible it may feel to overcome and undo all the misdirection, missteps, or flat out failures—having, being, and living success on your terms is always possible.

That bears repeating again.

No matter how far lost you feel.

No matter how unclear you are about what your SOULFIRE is.

No matter how elusive your drive is to fight for that faint memory of a dream.

If you are still on this side of Heaven.

If you are still alive.

You can have all that you desire.

IS YOUR SWITCH ON OR OFF?

SOMETIMES THE FULFILLMENT OF THESE DREAMS HAPPENS WHEN YOU DON'T REALLY WANT TO SAY "YES."

Before speaking became the go-to-thing for entrepreneurs to do, I was a speaker. I love speaking to audiences about NEURO HUMAN BRANDING, INTELLIGENT INFLUENCE, and seeing the light bulbs go on when they realize, "Yes, I am a luxury brand!"

For the most part, my speaking events were one-off experiences. A national conference here, a paid bonus workshop for an organization, the branding expert at a high-end coaching weekend event—I was known for these events as the go-to-branding speaker, but the event only happened once a year. And I wanted more.

Well, as life would have it, the opportunity for more came four months after my now ex-husband decided to leave. I was raw. I was emotional. I was just trying to figure life out again. Tory Johnson of Good Morning America's *Steals and Deals* fame had a multi city speaking tour called Spark and Hustle. I went to her multi-day event as an attendee and walked out as her tour's branding speaker for the rest of the cities.

A multi-city speaking tour is what I had always dreamed of, but it came at a time that keeping my emotions together was a challenge. Though logic would have said, "Pass up this opportunity and see if the invitation still stands next year," I said "Yes," immediately.

The tour was a great opportunity to prepare me for speaking anywhere and at any time so that I now can literally jump on stage with no notice and rock out a presentation. It was also great because it got me back on the road—and I love being on the road meeting my clients.

Yes, there were moments that were hard to deal with—like no one meeting me at the airport and coming home to an empty house. But saying "yes," turned on my passion for my field in a new way. Plus, it opened the doors to a three-year, multi-city speaking engagement, client relationships, and industry connections I would have had no other way.

You. Yes, you.

NO MATTER WHAT YOUR MIND, MOMMA,
MENTOR, OR ANYONE ELSE TELLS YOU- YOU
CAN HAVE, LIVE, BE, EMBODY, AND NEVER
LOSE ALL OF THE SUCCESS, INFLUENCE, GRACE,
FAVOR, AND NOTORIETY THAT YOU DESIRE.

It all begins with your willingness to CHOOSE to stop
playing mental, emotional, and social games The
OTHERS throw at you and to commit to your Soulfire
and the life of NEW NOTORIETY it brings.

LEARN.

Your definition of success is the only one that matters. Your definition needs to be clear, tactical, and tangible. Yes, it can have all the feelings, but you have to know when you have "made it."

DO.

There are many factors that either bring a trait forward or suppress it. If you aren't seeing the results you want, evaluate everyone and all things, which are around as well as inside of you. Just like with your DNA, having you go from struggle to success can be like flipping a switch.

BELIEVE.

Just because you haven't doesn't mean that you can't.

BECOME.

Let faith be the point from which everything you do, say, or think comes. Be a person who knows everything is possible.

CONNECT.

Surround yourself with people, books, trainings, shows—anything that stirs up a "Never say die." attitude. Use technology to your advantage to keep your mind focused on what you really want.

Chapter 24

HOW TO GO FROM STRUGGLE TO FLOW IN EVERY ASPECT OF YOUR LIFE

MAY YOU NEVER FORGET THAT EVERY DREAM, HOPE, AND DESIRE CAN BE YOUR REALITY IN AN INSTANT.

The idea about how to get from struggle to flow is an easy one. That is half the problem. We are programmed by The OTHERS that success takes lots of hard work and that alone carries with its numerous social stories on what equates to "hard work."

Is hard work blood, sweat, and tears?

Is hard work long hours, years, decades?

Is hard work manual labor where your body always hurts?

Is hard work one where you never see your family, you never have the relationships you really want, and always the one sacrificing for everyone else?

HOW YOU DEFINE "HARD WORK" DIRECTLY IMPACTS HOW YOU VIEW SUCCESS AND IS THE NUMBER ONE BLOCK TO GETTING INTO AND STAYING IN YOUR SOULFIRE FLOW.

Because yes, you can have a moment of brilliance, a flash of what this life should be, but it never lasts.

It doesn't last because you aren't capable of it. It doesn't last because your mindset and The OTHERS' social stories you hold around hard work stop you in your tracks. Sometimes it truly is solely you who is stopping yourself. And other times it is the infectious mindset of others that takes a hold of your good, intuitive, common sense.

MASS HYSTERIA MINDSET.

Many years ago, when Blackberry devices were the "in" type of phone, recording videos required real cameras, PowerPoint was still the beloved speaking presentation tool; it was a time when design portfolios were still on paper, and Justin Bieber was young and cute. It was a time to perfectly fit an experience I had with mass hysteria. Let me share with you one unbelievably memorable moment.

It was getting late into the evening hours and I was determined to get all the business "stuff" organized. Old client portfolio pieces, speaking props, event giveaways, product inventory for the various brands—you name it, I was determined to organize it. And though my branding business has always had a New York home, Arizona was headquarters from where everything was run.

In my organizational genius, I decided that the massive master closet in my Arizona home would be the perfect place to store all of this business stuff. I started cleaning out the closet, putting everything anywhere possible. Binders of previous client work were stacked in the tub. Speaking props were leaned up in my shower, of all places, and giveaways were stacked precariously high on the bathroom countertops.

I was in the ultimate organizational zone.

Then all of a sudden, I heard the doorbell ring. Well, I had no intention of answering. It was late. It was dark, and you guessed it, this happened way before video doorbells existed. Five minutes later the doorbell rang again—and again. Thirty minutes later I heard massive pounding on the front door even though I was all the way upstairs in the master bedroom closet minding my own organizational business.

I headed downstairs wondering, *What in the world is going on?* Turning on every light as I headed downstairs because I had no idea what was about to happen. I opened my front door. You can imagine what went through my mind: about thirty of my neighbors were scattered throughout my front yard and the cops were standing right in front of me.

Needless to say, I was shocked.

Then the cops asked me, "Miss, is someone in this house with you?"

I replied, "No, I am alone."

Then the cop said words, to this day I still can't believe, "Well, *ma'am* your neighbors here reported they saw a man in your upstairs window throw a rope around something, make a noose, and then hang himself. They claim they can see the body there now."

I then had to escort numerous police officers into my house, upstairs, and into my very messy in the midst of being organized master bathroom and closet. To show them that this "man" that had thrown a rope over something, made a noose and then hanged himself in the bathroom block glass window was simply a Justin Bieber cut out, which I used as a speaking prop, simply leaning up against the window.

No rope. No man. Just a cut out.

We then had to go back downstairs and tell all the neighbors how horribly wrong they were. Many of these neighbors were embarrassed, but some still believed what they claimed they saw.

EVEN WHEN WE TOOK JUSTIN OUT OF THE
WINDOW AND BROUGHT "HIM" DOWNSTAIRS
FOR THEM TO SEE—THEY DIDN'T BELIEVE THE
TRUTH. THEY BELIEVED THEIR MIND.

MYTH. MINDSET. THE MANY EXCUSES.

Now let's be honest, none of us like to admit we
hold ourselves back. How dare we be the ones doing
so? The OTHERS know this.

They know that pride will limit you from saying
anything about the matter and if you do say
anything, you will just blame your failure or lack of
success on them anyway. And, guess what, The
OTHERS are A-Okay with that.

They don't care if you use them as a scapegoat
because the more you do that, the more you don't
live your SOULFIRE or your life of NEW NOTORIETY.

THE MORE YOU BLAME THEM FOR YOUR OWN
FAILURES AND SHORTCOMINGS THE MORE
ALIVE YOU MAKE THE MYTH AND GIVE MORE
POWER TO THE MENTAL, EMOTIONAL,
PHYSICAL, AND SPIRITUAL STRONGHOLDS THE
OTHERS HAVE ON YOU AND SOCIETY
AT LARGE.

Yes, The OTHERS are the ultimate real-world Boogie Man. The Boogie Man will come out and get you, anytime, anywhere. You can't see him. You just sense him. And I don't know about you but the Disney Sunday movie about the Boogie Man still has me scared thirty years later. That is exactly what The OTHERS want. They want you scared, Yes, scared and running out of the proverbial room every time you turn off the lights.

You not taking personal responsibility does impact many more people than yourself. Your lack of responsibility feeds the beast—that in the end—is slowly destroying us. We are lobsters in the pot of water not realizing the heat is increasing moment-by-moment.

PAUSE FOR A SECOND AND RECOGNIZE THAT YOU—RIGHT NOW, WHERE YOU ARE—HAVE THE INFLUENCE AND POWER TO MAKE IT MORE OR LESS CHALLENGING FOR SOMEONE ELSE TO STEP INTO AND CONNECT WITH THEIR SOULFIRE SIMPLY BY CHOOSING TO ACKNOWLEDGE THE TRUTH ABOUT WHAT IS STOPPING YOU.

LEARN.
Your mind and imagination can either be your secret tools to ridiculous success—or never-ending sabotage.

DO.
Pause and honestly evaluate what is truly holding you back. The more that it is you, the better that is, because you can change yourself much easier and faster than an external situation that involves others.

BELIEVE.
Everything is possible.

BECOME.
Realize that your success goes far greater than you. When you are able to break free from the social stories and control of The OTHERS—you uplevel your life. But you also show everyone around what is possible in their own lives.

CONNECT.
Find ways to stay grounded in your SOULFIRE and DIVINE PARTNERSHIP on a daily basis. Some people use active journaling while others use guided meditation. When you find what ways make your partnership feel palatable you will be able to keep mental strength and clarity on point.

Chapter 25

WHY "THE LINE IN THE SAND OF SOON" LIFESTYLE IS KILLING YOUR SUCCESS AND THE DREAMS OF OTHERS

MAY YOU NEVER RETURN TO PLACES, PEOPLE, OR EXPERIENCES THAT DON'T SET YOUR SOUL ON FIRE.

Success is not optional.

In your mind you say it, in your heart you know it,
but somewhere in between the two, the line in the
sand always gets moved.

We say that tomorrow will be the day that we start
the new healthy lifestyle.

Tomorrow we start writing our book.

Tomorrow we will start making sales calls.

We draw a line in the sand of soon. Yet when
tomorrow comes we look at what we say we want,
erase that line and we push our dreams, goals, and
actions off to another day. We end up in the never-
ending loop of anticipation and possibilities.

THE DREAMS, LIVES, AND SUCCESS WE SAY WE WANT—THAT LIFE OF NEW NOTORIETY IS CLOSE AT HAND.

Twenty-four short little hours and everything will
be different. In twenty-four short little hours you
won't just be thinking about "what if" you will be
making it happen!

For those next twenty-four hours you can think,
imagine, daydream about all the beautiful
possibilities about how life will be different, better,
and what could be. For twenty-four hours you can
pacify that mental nagging and deep soul aching
that says, "I must take action." Because after all that
line in the sand is a mere twenty-four hours or less
away.

Similar to online dating and all of the dating apps, signing up for those services or "swiping right" makes you feel like you are doing something proactive to move your dream of finding the love of your life one step closer.

But when a match is finally made what do you do?

Either close the app in horror or ignore the connection all together. When presented with a possible answer to the dream you say you want, you move the line in the sand one more time.

The same holds true with living your SOULFIRE and being the Success Rebel, you say you want to be. When the time comes for you to step over that line and step up into your dreams, step up into living your SOULFIRE, step up into your DIVINE PARTNERSHIP, step up into a life of NEW NOTORIETY, life of success, influence, income, increase, and world changing impact—you simply buff that line away and reset it one more time.

Now you are thinking, *Come on, one time? That is no big deal. I needed to (*insert your logical excuse here*)*. You aren't feeling well. Your kids need you to do something for them. You need to make sure you can afford the project all the way through. You should do more industry research. The list of what logic, social stories and The OTHERS say you should do is endless. It just makes good common sense to buff this line in the sand away and push it off too soon.

BECAUSE SOON STILL FEELS GOOD. SOON GIVES YOU THE MENTAL HIGH WITHOUT THE PHYSICAL WORK. SOON IS MASTURBATING TO GET OFF ON THE IDEA VS. GOING ALL IN AND ACTUALLY DOING THE DEED.

WHY SAND SUCKS.

Lines in the sand of soon don't work because you don't do anything except waste time. You aren't taking effective action. You aren't being the hands and feet within your DIVINE PARTNERSHIP. You are simply being a bump on a log getting splinters up your ass.

And though not comfortable, it is what we have come to know. It is the cycle of life we have accepted for ourselves —sometimes knowingly— many times not. It is a pattern of life that the social stories and The OTHERS allow because they know you are all words and no action. So, in turn you are no threat.

Best of all, The OTHERS know that this pattern will actually discredit you and the idea of actually living your dreams, connecting with SOULFIRE and living your DIVINE PARTNERSHIP through a life of NEW NOTORIETY because you have cried "wolf" over and over again. No one believes you when and if the time finally comes.

Or you choose to follow antiquated social rules that make you feel like you are taking proactive true action; in the end that process fails you miserably because that is the exact way The OTHERS designed it.

Some of these rules are rooted in science gone wrong—like looking people straight in the eye or making sure you always give a firm handshake, which means you are confident. People misinterpret these "rules" such as staring them down like a rabid dog, or the firm handshake when you meet as trying to break their hand. Other times these rules are mere perceptions derived from pure fiction, like TV.

Do you remember the CBS TV show *How I Met Your Mother?*

On that show the playboy and ultimate ladies' man character, Barney Stinson had his Bro Code rules. This Bro Code book, yep it is an actual book you can buy, shares the 67 rules all guys need to know about picking up women, dumping women, and of course, always stay cool with the bros.

One of these Bro Codes is called the Naked Man. The Naked Man states that if a woman hasn't had sex with you by the third date, on the third date find a way to leave the room. When you return, be completely naked. And at that point she is bound to sleep with you.

OMG! Just writing out the details of the "rule" makes it sound ridiculously idiotic, but I have had it happen to me on three separate occasions with three separate guys.

Did these guys really think it was going to work?

Did they really think they were going to get lucky, get a relationship, find it endearing?

Did they really believe Barney's wisdom that there would be no way for a woman to resist a naked man that they barely know standing in front of them?

They answered that they didn't care what the true outcome was. They only cared that in their mind they checked off a box that said, "I tried. I tried to find a relationship. I tried to get laid. I tried. So, the issue isn't with me. It is with her." Ironically, they never see that the issues are with the rules The OTHERS created and they blindly followed.

Though blindly following arbitrary rules that don't work and only get the feel-good gold star is not a lifestyle pattern that any true Success Rebel would choose for themselves. There is a larger social ramification, which plays directly into the repression of others living their SOULFIRES. Because your line in the sand of soon lifestyle becomes proof that success never comes, that breaking free, living your SOULFIRE through a DIVINE PARTNERSHIP, having a life of influence, favor, and NEW NOTORIETY is not possible. It is not possible because they looked at you and you never did it—therefore nor can they.

Yes, the line in the sand of soon lifestyle is devastating for you. It is detrimental for generations of people you haven't met. You are influenced by this one simple, habitual, action. You don't want that for yourself or for others.

LINES IN CONCRETE.

Rid yourself of the idea and lifestyle option of the line in the sand of soon and realize that this is a line in concrete. That when you push off your dreams, when you push off taking action—being the hands and feet—in your DIVINE PARTNERSHIP, when you push off the favor and influence that comes with a life of NEW NOTORIETY you are setting into motion a bigger act of devastation than you realize.

So no, we are no longer drawing lines in the sand that can easily be moved. We are no longer writing our dreams and goals in pencil that can easily be erased. We are writing in concrete.

OUR MARK, OUR LOVE, THAT LIFE CHANGING MOMENT WHERE YOU HAVE DECIDED TO LEAVE THE SPLINTERY COMFORT OF THE OTHERS IS THERE FOR ALL TO SEE FOR ETERNITY.

There is no going back. Everyone, including yourself, will always and forever see your line in the concrete.

Now the choice is yours—whether that line is a reminder of the day you chose to fully step into your life of NEW NOTORIETY or if it is a haunting mark of dreams unfulfilled, DIVINE PARTNERSHIP wasted, and a life of mediocrely accepted. The choice is yours.

LEARN.

By lying to yourself you create self-sabotaging and reputational patterns that are more challenging to course correct than you are led to believe.

DO.

Become a person of raw honesty with yourself and others. Be honest about how much time something is going to take, if you are really going to come through, or what you really think about the situation. Radical honesty isn't about hurting others, it is about freeing your mind of the mental cobweb of control that keeps you from fully stepping into your Success Rebel status.

BELIEVE.

It is better to be truthful and free than kind and confined.

BECOME.

Start today being the "ink writer who does" not a pencil scheduler. Start today being the person who is known for their "Yes" meaning "Yes" and their "No" meaning "No."

CONNECT.

There will be moments when drawing lines in the concrete simply isn't fun. When you want to push back your deadline or forgive your friend who flaked on you one more time—every time you want to move the line in the concrete you have to ask yourself an honest "Why?" Was it because you miscalculated your time or is it because it isn't a priority?

Becoming a line in the concrete person with yourself, your business, and the people around you won't make you the most popular, but you will be unapologetically known for being a person of your word and consistent through and through.

And as with everything, find people to hang out with who also share these qualities. If it is through the Success Rebel Society or just with likeminded "getter done" types of peeps. Over time, the company you keep greatly impacts the consistency of your success and growth.

204

Chapter 26

THE PLAN FOR YOUR LIFE

MAY YOUR SOULFIRE ALWAYS BURN AS BRIGHT AS THE NORTH STAR.

We all have some plan for our lives. It may be just a few hours ahead but planning for what we think will be best for us is part of human nature.

The depth of our planning skills depends on who is living our life. When we make decisions from the conscious side of our brain, more autonomous long-term plans develop because we are looking to break free on what we feel is holding us back in our present lives. If we are purely under the domain of our subconscious mind then short term planning and more reactionary based fight or flight behavior is what happens.

It is this subconscious instinct that The OTHERS, social stories, and well-meaning loved ones take full advantage of when it comes to what your life should be. You get indoctrinated from childhood about who you should become, what your destiny will be, and ultimately, the success that will behold you.

For some of us, our loved ones hold lofty dreams that they wish they had fulfilled and in turn pass them down to you. For others, family obligation to go into the family business is the only way to happiness, success, and stay in the good graces of the family. And for others, the people who claimed to have loved us so no longer value the potential in who we really can be.

It is from these places that many of us plan our futures. We plan the priority of school in our lives. We plan what fields of study, groups, sports, trades we become part of, where we live, how we live, and who we associate with for the most part.

THIS IS ALL PLANNED FROM THE VANTAGE POINT OF SOMEONE ELSE'S EXPECTATION OF YOU. NOT YOUR OWN SOUL FELT, DIVINELY INSPIRED DESIRES.

Yet before the indoctrination began you had your version and vision of success. Now it may have been a two-year olds version, but the heart of what it meant to you still lives. The "reason" you felt it was success was there. It is in that innocence where the Divine intention of what sparks your SOULFIRE creates the undeniable magnetism, which your SOULFIRE is to you.

The art of becoming and being a Success Rebel is in sifting through everything in life The OTHERS, and anyone else has ever told you verbally or experientially. Then deciding whether this is your Divine truth—your SOULFIRE. Or is this the expectation, social story, or intention of someone else?

DECIPHERING WHAT IS AND IS NOT YOURS IS ACTUALLY EASY. THE PROBLEM IS WHETHER YOU WILL LISTEN AND ACT ON THE ANSWER YOU RECEIVE?

Have you watched the Netflix series *Tidying Up* with Marie Kondo or read the book *The Life-Changing Magic of Tidying Up* by Marie Kondo? Marie Kondo is passionate about organization and keeping only the items that spark joy, as she says, *To discover this, you are asked to hold the item close to your chest and ask yourself "Does this bring me joy?" If the answer is "no" you are supposed to donate the item. If the answer is "yes" you get to keep the item.*

But as you have seen if you are a fan of her Netflix series, many people have their initial answer, but then apply the logic of The OTHERS to the situation.

- What if I may need this again?
- It is still in good condition; I shouldn't be wasteful.

- Someone special gave it to me and they would be upset if they found out I got rid of it.

In the end the very people who had their "answer" lost it in the social stories and logical maze of The OTHERS. Which leaves them feeling like a failure, more confused, and reinforcing the story that no matter if they try, they will not succeed. Check, check, and check—for The OTHERS keep ownership of your mind and mess.

ORGANIZING YOUR PRIORITIES.

Discovering or rediscovering what is the plan for your life is actually very similar to a well-known Japanese organizational technique. Simply think about the task, the relationship, the work and ask yourself "Does it make me happy?" And wait for the response.

Sometimes it is a physical response of joy, excitement in your chest, a smile or feeling the pressure on your shoulders pushing you down. Other times it is a sense of peace, calm, happiness, or dread. And sometimes you can even hear the answer within your internal thoughts.

But like with Marie Kondo's organizational technique, the first answer is generally the right answer. And just like with organizing—it is so easy and sometimes instantly in which the social stories and self-condemnation from The OTHERS begin to pile on.

- You have spent hundreds of thousands of dollars getting this education you must be a (insert profession here.)

- You have been in this industry for years. It doesn't make sense to start a new career now.

- You are lucky you have a job, don't be selfish by wanting more.

TO BE A SUCCESSFUL SUCCESS REBEL YOU HAVE TO BE ABLE TO CONTROL YOUR MIND AND EMOTIONS BECAUSE IN THE END THAT CONTROLS YOUR MONEY.

The first step in controlling your mind and emotions is how you spend your time. You are never going to be a success at anything if it isn't truly your heart and goal.

The sad truth is that you may believe your own voice more than that of anyone else—an annoying running internal dialogue about how you really see yourself in success and life. All those negative thoughts don't just psyche you out in the moment, they actually make the memory of your failure or the fear of potential failure much bigger in your brain. Allowing these negative thoughts to come up faster, easier, and over and over again is a given—unless you choose to stop them.

Your subconscious mind, though brilliant on so many levels, doesn't look at what logically makes sense. It doesn't care what your logical mind says you want today. It listens to your past experiences, and the countless internal dialogue of fear, negativity, and unworthiness you have fed it all these years.

Your subconscious mind simply wonders if the situation at hand is unsafe, will cause you harm, or will produce a situation that goes against who and what you have always said that you were.

The subconscious mind stores every experience you have ever had, whether that experience actually happened to you or one you just thought about. Yes, the subconscious mind doesn't know the difference between imagination and reality. All of those stories, movies and tv shows, which portray the struggle to make it, the "man" always kicking the little guy when he is down, the woman who can never find the love of her life—to your subconscious mind it happened to you and in turn will recreate similar ideas as your future reality

But you don't have to be controlled by your subconscious mind.

YOU CAN ACTUALLY USE YOUR IMAGINATION AND ITS BLIND-DOGGED DETERMINATION TO CREATE WHAT YOU SAY YOU WANT TO YOUR ADVANTAGE...ONCE YOU ACKNOWLEDGE THE POWERHOUSE OF POTENTIAL IT REALLY IS.

You are smarter than you think and more capable than you realize. If you are here on this earth, you are fully able to pause the patterns that have been your life and decide to choose again.

LEARN.

Success only comes when truth is at the foundation.

DO.

Get ridiculously honest about how you want your life to go. Clear out subconscious stories that are holding you back. Take conscious effort to begin to use your subconscious mind to your full advantage.

BELIEVE.

Believe what you say you want and who you say you are.

BECOME.

Guard your heart and your mind from frivolous social stories that may seem benign but go against the life you want to lead, how you view yourself, and how you see the work of your SOULFIRE.

CONNECT.

Like with all life changing transformations, you have to surround yourself with people and social stories that support your perspective. Recovering alcoholics don't go back and hang out in bars. And people looking to live their SOULFIRE, become an influencer and live a life of NEW NOTORIETY can't hang out with the same people that create the subconscious mental blocks that were stopping them in the first place.

Chapter 27

PAUSE, PLAN AND PIVOT

MAY YOU ALWAYS KNOW THAT YOU ARE NEVER STUCK. THERE IS ALWAYS A SOLUTION.

No one has lived one day on this side of Heaven and had the perfect life-experience. No matter how magical the day may have been, if you think long and hard enough you can find a few things that could have made that moment even better.

If we can think of ways we could have improved the best days of our lives, think of what the impact we could have if we would pause, plan, and pivot with regards to a lifetime of days?

You are reading this book because you know and want your life to be radically different than where it is right now. To make such a change you must pause, plan, and pivot.

No, it isn't about trashing everything in your life and starting from scratch in everything. Such radical behavior is the number one way to not follow through or succeed.

Pause, Plan, and Pivot is about recognizing and course correcting where you have gotten off track from your SOULFIRE, DIVINE PARTNERSHIP, and the life of grace, success, influence, and NEW NOTORIETY you are meant to live. Then, to consciously pivot and take action with new clarity, intention, purpose, and in partnership.

Like all the "rules" in this book, the hardest part isn't taking action it is trusting yourself that your instinct was right, sound, and accurate for you.

BUT WHEN DONE RIGHT THE PAUSE, PLAN, AND PIVOT METHOD TRANSFORMS.

Businesses that were barely making it grow 300-400% not just one year or two years—but for a decade and beyond.

Brands that use to be reliant on only one stream of income diversify smartly and now have seven profitable streams.

Marriages on the brink of divorce turn into true love feasts that would make even teenagers blush.

Some of the greatest solutions come from the simplest methods. Pause, Plan, and Pivot is one of those.

Let's be honest. It's easy to get alone with your thoughts for a few days, decompress, and evaluate what is and is not working for you. Even deciding on the new direction is simple enough. But it is in those moments of deciding to pivot that we fail to fly.

FLIP. FLOP. FEAR.

For my brands, I call these moments "Flip, Flop, Fear." Your brand gets off the track to success goals and purposes as well. Because after all, brands are built by people, for people, and with the flaws of people built right in.

Most companies hire a branding agency like mine to get them back on track or to build them right from the start. We take care of the pause, the plan, decide on the pivot—but in the end the actual act of moving forward in that new agreed upon direction is the sole choice and responsibility of the client.

I wish I could tell you that "Flip, Flop, Fear" wasn't common, but it is. Branding is a deeply personal experience, when done right. The subconscious triggers within the client always come out. On Season 1 of the international award-winning hit reality TV Show, *Fix My Brand With Ali Craig*, we had one such brand.

This woman's empowerment brand was set to be one of the best transformations of the season. All along the way, the client was all "in." She was outwardly proactive about the change and the new direction. Yes, she loved the Plan and the Pivot—until she had to walk the walk.

Literally one day before the launch of the website, offers, and everything—the client freaked out. She freaked out about the brand, being on the show, everything. What social stories triggered her to throw away months of hard work, an amazing marketing opportunity, plus brand reach she said she wanted? Like how many licks it takes to get to the center of a Tootsie Pop—the world may never know.

Some people trash their new brands, others trash their income streams so that they can't afford to stay in business, others invest idiotically in frivolous products or services they don't need. But no matter how it shows up—the "why" is always because of fear.

It is in these very moments that the rush of social stories, societal pressures, and the hauntings of The OTHERS comes rushing around. Instead of recognizing the illusion of fear that is in front of them, they want to reverse all of their decisions and return to what is known—even when it isn't working.

As the expression goes, "It is better to keep the devil you know, than risk meeting a new one."

Doesn't that expression just reek of The OTHERS suppression tactics? Ugh!

How do you win?

How do you course correct?

How do you keep going?

Easy, by staying consciously aware of the game being played and not fall for disruptive tactics. Learn the plays of your opponents. Then set out to play YOUR game.

DON'T JUST CHANGE YOUR PLAYS, CHANGE THE RULES. THAT'S HOW YOU MASTER AND EXECUTE THE PAUSE, PLAN, AND PIVOT.

LEARN.

The simplest solutions can create radical results when purposeful action is taken.

DO.

Commit yourself to being solution-focused vs. method-focused. Be open to the creative ideas that Pause, Plan, and Pivot can give you: the "how" to bring your voice and the work of your DIVINE PARTNERSHIP into the world.

BELIEVE.

Success is just a solution away.

BECOME.

Become known for being a solutionist person; when you see the solutions, you see the possibilities.

CONNECT.

Being solution minded is a mindset you have to train your brain to see. Play Sudoku and other problem-solving games. Personally, my favorite app for this is called Lumosity. It has been around for years. They have a variety of games to help keep your mind sharp and your solution focused brain on point.

Chapter 28

WHY YOU SHOULD BE LIKE EINSTEIN

MAY YOU ALWAYS KNOW THAT REBELS ARE MEANT TO BE REVOLUTIONARY.

Black sheep, prodigal sons, or wayward souls—every culture has their version of the somewhat acceptable outlaws. You know, the one that doesn't quite follow the rules, but isn't the cave dwelling, naked man either.

From these black sheep social stories, we have been taught to never want to be such a horrible thing. That in doing so your life will be an utter failure, full of struggle and pain, and in the end you won't find happiness, love, fulfillment, or acceptance.

Many of us find ourselves there at some point in our lives. Some from an early age know that what is acceptable to the masses isn't acceptable to the souls that we are and therefore the struggle of who we should be is a constant battle. For others, life presents us with a choice at those pivotal moments to follow our heart or mass mentality of The OTHERS.

Now society would tell us that the way of the black sheep would lead to death, yet that simply isn't the case.

Though the social stories talk about being devil possessed, or an antichrist, I have found that many Black Sheep are simply Success Rebels in sheep's clothing.

FROM BLACK SHEEP TO SUCCESS REBEL.

After working with and training entrepreneurs, founders, and thought leaders from around the world for over two decades, I can tell you it is the black sheep rebels that make bank. The black sheep are the Success Rebels.

Granted, black sheep rebels aren't going to be successful by common social standards. They are going to be the ones who help us evolve, revolutionize industries, and change the way we see the world.

In the past, many of these rebels were artists, philosophers, scientists, and inventors. Einstein, van Gogh, Tesla, Plato, Curry, Aristotle, Newton, and Picasso—all of these greats changed the way we now see art, science, and life. All of these greats were considered a bit eccentric, untraditional black sheep, and total Success Rebels. But what does this list also show us?

It shows us how to be a black sheep, break the repression of The OTHERS, and overcome the social stories to make bank. It also shows that throughout the ages, and yes, we are talking centuries here, the black sheep stories are viewed as slightly less threatening to The OTHERS. We aren't being burnt at the stake or dying in fits of madness anymore, but we are also not widely beloved unless we know how to work the system.

WORKING THE OTHERS TO YOUR ADVANTAGE.

How does a black sheep make bank? You have to play the game of Einstein not Tesla.

Both brilliant minds who have forever changed the way we see the world. But Einstein knew the moves of The OTHERS and used their tactics against themselves by changing the game that was truly being played. The following three ideas represent the distinction.

1. PLAY UP YOUR WEIRD.

Einstein didn't try to fit in. He didn't apologize about his appearance, brilliance, or demeanor. On many levels he used his eccentric ways to play up the social story The OTHERS desired.

WHEN IT COMES TO BRANDS, I ALWAYS SAY THERE IS WISDOM AND WEALTH IN THEIR BEING WEIRD. YES, SOME OF OUR GREATEST IDEAS AND ELEMENTS OF CONNECTION CAN OCCUR WHEN WE SPEAK FROM AN UNFILTERED HEART.

But by visually expressing our weird, be it through our clothes, our untamed hair, or hair color for that matter, we force The OTHERS to put us into the box of misfit people. Meaning that because we don't fit their social norms, we have to be individually inspected to see where we fit.

PLAYING UP YOUR BEING WEIRD GETS YOU A SECOND LOOK.

2. NEVER WAIVER ON THE BRILLIANCE YOU AND YOUR DIVINE PARTNERSHIP BRING.

Einstein owned what he brought to the table and didn't fall for the false humility social story as Tesla did. Many people fall for the humility trap because people fundamentally want to be good people. Plus, true humility and living in a DIVINE PARTNERSHIP go hand in hand. So, it only seems natural to be humble.

But as soon as The OTHERS know your weak point, a desire for humility and what that social perception means, you are done. Because they know how to trigger you into always backing down, always not taking that next step or big leap. In your attempt to be of service, The OTHERS will use that to limit your ability to serve.

3. ONLY BE AROUND BRILLIANCE.

Einstein surrounded himself with people who either saw his works as valuable and brilliant or his personal value and brilliance.

Black sheep and Success Rebels rarely have tons of true friends surround them because the majority of people don't understand their brilliance. But Success Rebels know that the company you keep influences your ability to create, show up, and own the space unapologetically.

A FIGHTER'S MINDSET.

To me the perfect modern example of all of this in action is former UFC fighter Angela Magaña.

If you don't know Angela's story here is the 150 word or less version.

Angela was born to a mom addicted to heroin. Living on the streets of LA with her mom and baby sister—Magaña didn't know that this was not a normal life. From a young age though, she knew that she was meant to do more, be better, and that anything she wanted in life was possible.

Fast forward through the years where she experienced her Mexican father being deported, being raped when she was 14 years old by the father of a child she was babysitting (while his wife watched) and her mother dying of an overdose when she was 17 years old—Magaña found the MMA Cage as well as the boxing ring. She used them to focus her energy on being the best.

For over 15 years, Magaña has been the best in and out of the ring. Professionally she is one of the rare MMA fighters who can financially support themselves with their career. She built a gym in Puerto Rico to train the next generation of fighters and support the Puertorriqueñas community.

Angela has overcome and mastered so much. But what she has truly mastered is knowing that her mind is her money maker. Not how smart she is; not how manipulative she can be. The mastery lies within her: her actions, thoughts, reactions, body—and her mind is at the very heart of it.

I was fortunate enough to interview this amazing woman for a show my production company, Entreventure, creates called EmpiHER TV. As any good interviewer does, I did my homework to brush up on exactly who this 11/10 fighter was.

Angela beats The OTHERS at their own game every time. She is the Einstein of her industry and makes bank doing that in just three simple actions.

1. She is crystal clear on her gifts.

2. She remains unapologetic about her choices.

3. She doesn't live by trash talk; what she says is truly how she sees the world.

With no need for a false sense of humility, Angela is perfectly clear about who she is even if The OTHERS say differently. This savvy entrepreneur goes as far as to intentionally use The OTHERS offense to her games advantage by playing up her "bad girl" "queen" image.

Of course, Angela controls who is around her, her family, and her fighters. She understands that mindset is everything, and just how other people around you affect your mindset more than you know.

If you want to hear about Angela's story and outlook on life, you can watch her full episode on Apple Tv's Notoriety Network or the network's app called The NEW NOTORIETY available in the IOS and Google Play stores.

LEARN.

You may not be able to control how others behave, but you control the game you play.

DO.

Being a Success Rebel isn't always about fighting the "good fight" against The OTHERS. Sometimes it is using their own game to your advantage. Begin to look at the game they are trying to play with you and see how you can use it to your advantage.

BELIEVE.

If you control your mind, you control your destiny.

BECOME.

Learn how to take a step back and evaluate objectively the moves you are making. Are you leaving yourself open in a certain area? Not coming across as powerful as you could be with the impressions you are making? Allowing others to marginalize you in some way?

By learning how to take the mental step back from any given situation, you can wisely orchestrate the moves you make and how you can use the moves of The OTHERS against themselves.

CONNECT.

Yes, being a Success Rebel can be exhausting. Sometimes you just need real human interaction. This is why with both the Success Rebel Society and the Success Rebel CEO Life group we have in person experiences and meet ups all around the world. They are great ways to grow, learn, and simply chill in like mindedness.

Chapter 29

HOW TO WIN AT ANYTHING

MAY YOU NEVER LOSE SIGHT OF YOUR "WHY" BECAUSE YOU BECOME OBSESSED WITH YOUR "HOW."

For the most part we focus our idea of success on one action or area. We are taught to goal plan, schedule and work towards that one business goal or that one personal goal. That the only way to succeed is to be laser focused on the one area— that's it.

This single mindedness even happens in random situations that occur in everyday life.

A few years back, I was standing in line waiting to board my Southwest flight to LA. I was dressed casual chic. Jeans, blazer, tee and because the destination was LA, I was wearing a pair of sandal heels.

Now if you are unfamiliar with Southwest Airlines, you don't have an assigned seat. You have an assigned boarding position. I was A1. So yes, I was standing at the front of the line.

While standing there waiting for them to start general boarding, a man approaches me. He came in really close, mouth to my ear, hand on my shoulder and says to me, "I just have to tell you, I find your feet soooo sexy!"

Say WHAT?!?!

Then this complete stranger just walks away.

Clearly this fellow passenger had a very focused mind on something, and it wasn't the fact that he was in a public situation about to board a plane. A one-track-mind can run you into the proverbial brick wall if you aren't paying attention.

BE A CHARIOT DRIVER NOT A ONE-HORSE RIDER.

Like in branding, niching your goals or focuses down to one thing may sound logical. But like everything The OTHERS create, it fails to consider the holistic nature of humanity. No matter if we are talking about Human Needs Psychology, NEURO HUMAN BRANDING, or NERI Profiling (Neuro

Emotional Relationship Intelligence.) Human beings aren't singular. We are multi spectrum.

WE ARE MULTI SPECTRUM. WE DON'T JUST WANT MONEY, SUCCESS, OR FAME. THERE IS AN INTENTION OR "WHY" BEHIND THE WANT.

We also don't just see success as personal or professional. Because when we do, we fail to fully commit and in turn don't receive the full success, influence, or life of NEW NOTORIETY that is due us.

This is why when we look to make conscious growth while working within our DIVINE PARTNERSHIP, we must plan in a way that targets our SOULFIRE—and in turn—the life of NEW NOTORIETY that it brings.

ALWAYS ON POINT.

The idea of SOUL TARGETING came to me years ago on the gun range. I was stressed out trying to manage all of my businesses' growing pains, client work, and my personal goals. Every traditional goal setting method fell short. Light bulb! I was not trying to push one goal setting ball up the proverbial hill. I was trying to push many at one time.

I came to the gun range with my Type A mind on everything else. As my gun instructor, Jon, and I started shooting, I was getting frustrate because I was not hitting the target exactly where I intended.

I was close, but never spot-on to where I was aiming.

Jon told me to stop focusing on the precise point I was aiming for and to create a mental box around what I was going for. This way as long as I hit within the box, that was a "win." Once I gave myself a mental frame for what was acceptable for me to claim as an appropriate hit to the target, low and behold, I actually started hitting the precise point I so desperately tried to achieve earlier.

Then it hit me. The same holds true with our goals.

When we are overly focused on being so specific with our goals, we don't see the win when we are slightly off. I remember not celebrating when my second book became a 3x bestseller simply because my goal was for a 5x bestseller book.

I took this new perspective on targeting and started testing it out on my SOULFIRE, work, projects, and even working on my private branding clients' work. I utilize it as a litmus test for what to say "Yes" or "No" to.

And just like my experience on the gun range, goals which were initially challenging, ultimately became an easy flow.

NOW I BECAME SPOT ON BECAUSE I WAS NO LONGER OBSESSED WITH ONE SINGLE POINT.

Instead I created a framework for every single soul target that measures personal and professional success for me while creating a guide to how to actually accomplish the goal.

Three years out, I am living, teaching, and working this method and the results are crazy. Five-year goals are achieved in 18 months. TV shows my production company, Entreventure, has created aren't just award winning—they are international award-winning multiple times over. Branding clients' bottom lines aren't increasing by minute amounts each year, they are multiplying exponentially.

TRUE SUCCESS ISN'T ABOUT BEING SOLELY FOCUSED ON A MANUFACTURED GOAL, IT IS ABOUT BEING HOLISTICALLY FOCUSED ON THE TOTAL IMPACT, INFLUENCE, AND INTENTION OF YOUR SOULFIRE AND DIVINE WORK.

LEARN.

You are multifaceted and what you pursue should be too. Sticking to one area for the sake of following the rules will lead to your failure.

DO.

Stop focusing on the one. The one way to succeed. The one way to make money. The one way to find one. Create the framework necessary to make sure you win in all areas of your life, while still achieving the primary goal you are going after.

BELIEVE.

"How" success shows up is less important than "why" it appears.

BECOME.

Become obsessed with your vision. Don't let anyone limit your reach, scope, or influence simply because that isn't "industry standard." Change the standard, change the industry, uplevel your influence.

CONNECT.

Many times, Success Rebels use their SOULFIRES and DIVINE PARTNERSHIPS not just as ways to change the world, but revenue-makers as well. To keep such growth up in a high intensity-low competition manner becomes a challenge when you work solo.

The challenge of working solo is one reason why, along with developing a production company, we also created Success Rebel CEO Life. This intimate in person group is a marketing, media, and influence-building program. But the byproduct is a community of driven success rebels who inspire, spark ideas, and encourage—but don't compete.

Chapter 30

SEX, LOVE, AND DISRUPTION

MAY YOU NEVER FORGET THE POWER OF CONSISTENCY.

One hit wonders—15 minutes of fame, insta-celebrity—speed isn't just how we see and do life, it is how we see influence, status, and success. We live in a society that promotes instant influence; that anyone can be an expert or influencer, well, instantly. Numbers, followers, likes, and retweets is what we are taught as the mark of influence and in turn success status.

THE TRUTH IS THAT INSTANT NEVER CREATES LONG TERM INCOME.

Work in an industry long enough and you see this reality. The fancy new company, product, or service; an innovative new approach that is going to take the world by storm. Each may be the next best thing or may be dead and buried as fast as it came roaring in and disrupting the industry standards.

DISRUPTION.

The idea of the Rebel has always been the antithesis in The OTHERS' stories. They have done everything to scare people away from being, doing, or even thinking about being a rebel in any manner.

From biker gangs to tattoo covered individuals, anything other than strait-laced was viewed and labeled rebellious, dangerous, and deadly. If society as a whole begins to investigate these stories a bit deeper, they will realize that the lies The OTHERS have always told about such Rebels, well are that, lies. It's not like The OTHERS are going to get in trouble for such lies, anyway.

What is to be said about the biker gangs who now escort children of abuse to their court cases so they can feel protected and defended in some of the most vulnerable times in their lives? Tattoos are socially acceptable even in some of the most traditional business industries.

Being a disrupter was previously the ultimate way to get kicked out of the tribe, but now it is the way to stay in.

The social stories of The OTHERS don't always stay stagnant. And just as everything else in life has sped up in our modern lives, so has the rewriting of these social stories to keep society under wraps.

DISRUPTERS ARE NOW PRAISED AS BUSINESS GENIUSES.

What about Uber, DoorDash, and AirBnB? Other disruptors in society are looked at as the good guys, as we look to Snowden and the Wikileaks founder, Julian Assange. And even more disrupters of social basics, such as who can and cannot play certain sports, use certain restrooms, or wear certain clothes.

It is not that these businesses, people, or policies are good or bad. But they have created a new enemy within our lifetime. The bad guy isn't to be the Rebel anymore. The new bad guy will embrace the challenge to be the one that doesn't change because society says so.

But your soul purpose won't change.

Your DIVINE PARTNERSHIP won't change.

Your heart and passion won't change.

Yes, you may change the way you show up, but the "why" is always there. So, in short, the core of who you are, why you were created won't change just because society may say differently.

So, stay alert.

Leaders must stay alert. As a success Rebel you are a leader, an alpha, a protector of your SOULFIRE and the people you are meant to serve. You must be alert to every changing cultural shift that The OTHERS are unleashing.

This knowledge isn't so that you CAN CHANGE, but it is so that you can then consciously CHOOSE HOW it is best to engage in all of your relationships.

- How can you better utilize NEURO HUMAN BRANDING by understanding which social stories are now being triggered?

- How can you meet your audience where they are? By authentically using NERI to understand their human needs and fears—and your own.

- How can you use your energy and influence intelligently, with methods from the International Society of Intelligent Influence, to de-escalate or explore the nature of a situation?

THE TORTOISE AND THE HARE.

Let's be honest, INSTANT is sexy. Do you remember the children's story *The Tortoise And The Hare*? Even though the moral of the story was to be more like the Tortoise, everyone wanted to be the Hare. I know I did.

The Hare was cool and fast. The Hare was a bit of a playboy and seemed to be able to convince anyone of anything. The Hare is who our society and The OTHERS really teach us to be.

INSTANT CREATES EGO AND A FALSE PERCEPTION OF WHAT SUCCESS IS AND WHAT IT TAKES TO GET THERE.

Instant isn't replicable which means it is not sustainable by yourself or others. The OTHERS know this, but they also know that instant is so attractive as well.

Instant is attractive because we know it isn't supposed to happen. Therefore, because it did happen we must be pretty darn special. Playing on our human needs for variety, significance, growth, and love—the idea of instant with all of its pitfalls and whatnots is still highly attractive.

Fame, fortune, ego, and pride are what the idea of instant plays to. The OTHERS know this. They also know that these "sins" are the ultimate no-no's for humanity because they are so hard to come back from—for yourself and your reputation. It's rather like getting a tattoo while you are drunk. Sounds like a great idea at the moment, but it is very difficult to walk that mistake back long term.

The OTHERS know this and they do everything in their power to frustrate you into thinking you aren't growing fast enough, wonder why you are the IT person of the moment, and working your bum trying to "go viral" in the hopes of getting your shot. The OTHERS position on your efforts toward the unknown and away from THE DIVINE PARTNERSHIP that will get you known.

When as a Success Rebel you focus on your SOULFIRE heart and the DIVINE PARTNERSHIP, your work creates a place where magic can happen. Connections are made, doors are opened, and what once looked impossible—is possible. Not because of numbers, algorithms, trends, or you—but because of the spark that was created when your work and the world combined.

But this all takes time. The greatest fires aren't started in an instant. They burn slowly and deep and then grow and build. Studies show that to gain "instant expert" status you have about 18-21 years of working your work. And a true expert has over 100 hours of training in their industry to truly be viewed as an expert.

SEX AND LOVE.

The idea of instant plays on our innate human need for variety, but consistency feels like a not so sexy counterpart. Instant is a quickie. Consistency is Karma Sutra.

Consistency in how you show up.

Consistency in your message.

Consistency in your outlook, energy, and intention.

Consistency when you think no one is watching and when you know everyone is.

Consistency when life is good and whenever fear is coming your way.

Consistency doesn't just create cash flow, it creates connections, relationships, and true influence.

PEOPLE ARE ABLE TO TRUST YOU AND WHAT YOU SAY BECAUSE THEY KNOW YOU HAVE BEEN AROUND AND WILL BE AROUND.

And it is those moments when you think this will be life, day in and day out. Then the Divine strikes you, All that consistent work and influence, create prominence and the sought-after life of NEW NOTORIETY that you have always wanted.

Yes, the idea of being the modern-day tortoise doesn't seem to jive with the sexy cool, Success Rebel vibe. But when you realize how sexy cool it is to not play into the hands of The OTHERS, you realize that consistency may be slow and steady work, but the life changing moments happen in an instant—when you aren't focused on instant influence.

LEARN.

The meaning of social stories and stereotypes change based on the needs of The OTHERS. The same holds true about the quickie of influence, income, and instant success. Consistency, the Karma Sutra of success, is where growth, true influence, and the life of NEW NOTORIETY come from.

DO.

Commit to the long-term game, the long-term success, and the long-term influence which will gain you the relationships, influence, and success you want.

BELIEVE.

Consistency in the end wins.

BECOME.

Your SOULFIRE won't be fully realized in a day. Learn the art of pivoting from the big vision, goals, and dreams you have—and the steps you know when done consistently will get you there. Within your DIVINE PARTNERSHIP, you are the hands and feet, so trying to sprint to the finish line will only leave you worn out. Be inspired by the overarching mission of your SOULFIRE and commit to take one step forward to it every day.

CONNECT.

It is hard to feel consistent when you feel like you are taking two steps forward and three steps back. Many times, it isn't the problems in the physical world that stop you. It is the influence of The OTHERS energy and attacks from the spiritual world that slow you down to a crawl.

I have always been a big proponent for Prayer Warriors. Prayer Warriors are a group of people who are dedicated to praying for you, your business, your relationships, your life overall. Personally, I find that most Success Rebels tend to have an empathic side to their personality. Therefore, negative feelings, emotions, and energies can get them off track. And creating a hard-shell exterior blocks these rebels from their true brilliance.

This is where the Prayer Warriors come in.

And it is one reason why every month in the Success Rebel Society, I lead a live Prayer Warrior call where we pray for and over each other's SOULFIRE, while sharing the success stories that have occurred along the way.

5

BE UTTERLY SELFISH TO BE OF SERVICE AND A SUCCESS

Chapter 31

INSTANT SUCCESS THROUGH ENERGETIC INCOME

MAY YOU ALWAYS KNOW THAT YOUR TRUE CURRENCY AND VALUE IS IN THE ENERGY YOU BRING.

Discovering and partnering with your SOULFIRE so that you can live a life of NEW NOTORIETY doesn't fully happen overnight. Not that it isn't possible, but the truth is we couldn't handle it if it did.

The blessing, and sometimes frustration, of tapping into your SOULFIRE and in turn, your life of NEW NOTORIETY, is that it just takes one thought, one moment, one spark. The tides, the struggle, the frustration—all can truly change in an instant.

Change by change, moment by moment. They may seem innocuous, but these changes do happen, and the snowball of success occurs faster and faster when your energy is in alignment with the true intentions of you living your SOULFIRE.

Believe it—your energy defines everything.

THE SPINNING WHEEL OF LIFE.

Remember the type of energy that would overtake you when it was recess time at school? No matter what type of kid you were, book nerd to social butterfly, everyone loved recesses. And as a Gen Xer, my generation was still lucky enough to have the cool, and potentially deadly, playground equipment.

You remember the dome of bars that you could crawl up, over, and all around in?

And what about the carousel merry-go-round? Or as I always thought of it the spinning wheel of death.

I don't know about you, but the merry-go-round on my school's playground was awesome and so wrong at the same time. We would all pile on the merry-go-round, people standing in the center and everyone reaching to hold to the bar for dear life.

Then the rest of the kids would start spinning the carousel. Faster and faster it would go until it hit a point where the entire base of the merry-go-round would get unstable and wobble. This is when the kids riding the merry-go-round who were

unfortunate to be the last ones on were falling
down. Barely holding on so they didn't shoot out of
the carousel and land on the hard ground.

When the ride would finally stop how you felt would
greatly depend on a few factors.

Did you lose your grip and slide right off?

Did you stay standing, but couldn't walk in a
straight line and your lunch wasn't going to stay
down either?

Or were you the first one in the center—right at
the core of the carousel and you had the time of
your life? Wind whipping through your hair, lots
of happy screams and laughs?

How you enjoyed the merry-go-round ride was
greatly based on where you positioned yourself, who
was or was not around you, and who or what
controlled how fast you could spin.

The same holds true with your energy.

MENTAL BLOCKS, EMOTIONAL STRONGHOLDS, AND SOCIAL STORIES CAN ALL SLOW DOWN YOUR RATE OF SPEED.

But just like when you were a kid, going a bit slower
wasn't really all that bad. What was worse was when
you went so fast that in the end you couldn't stand
straight.

This can happen with your energy as well. You can be doing all the right things but all of a sudden the outside forces of The OTHERS can affect your ride. These blocks affect your energy, but they can also affect your biology too which in turn will affect your energetic levels and presence.

TOPLESS AT MY DESK.

Social patterns are one of the easiest ways that The OTHERS stop us from owning our full energetic power and from using our biology to our SOULFIRE's advantage.

Wake up at this time.

Go to bed at this time.

These days are for only this type of work.

You can only eat at this time, poop at this time, and f**k at this time.

It doesn't matter if that doesn't work for you, your natural biorhythms, energetic flows, or life.

There are social stories about people who stay up late, wake up late, eat late. In short it is never that it is the late person who gets anything good, but more that the social patterns of time, decorum, and daily habits go far beyond being a night owl.

To fully embrace your SOULFIRE, energetic flow, and in turn the audience changing impact, influence, and life of NEW NOTORIETY that comes with it—you truly have to do you. Which sounds pretty simple, until you actually try.

Consider the looks of shock and awe you get when you tell someone you don't drink alcohol simply because you don't. Or the simple limitations on your options for yoga classes or grooming appointments if you wake up at 10AM. Or pure anger when you buy your shoes in the kids' section, simply because they fit and are $15 cheaper.

WHO ARE YOU!?!

People's initial reaction when you go against many societal standards is shock and disgust, mainly because you choose to go against the fiber of what creates order and feeds their innate human need for consistency. Most rebels are OK with this, but it can be a challenge for the relationships you keep.

As you know, healthy, fulfilling relationships are essential for you to live, produce and be your best. Having open, clear communication with the ones you love about their needs and yours is essential.

Maybe you can't make it to your kid's basketball games because they play so late and you naturally awake during the Divine hours—2 to 4AM—to work. But you can bring your kid to school and watch some of the early morning practices, or practice hoops together on the weekend.

THERE IS ALWAYS A SOLUTION TO EVERY EXPERIENCE OR SITUATION.

As the Success Rebel leader that you are, it is your job to lead the pack in finding solutions, which can be completed with grace and ease when your energy is in the right spot.

YOUR ENERGY IS YOUR CURRENCY.

We all know that when we bring the right energy to our relationships, work, and life things just flow better. The experiences are more impactful and positive, and they create the lasting memories we hope for. Though The OTHERS have deemed this acceptable to think about this on a personal level, bringing this energy into business or your life's work is strictly forbidden.

BUT THE TRUTH IS THAT OUR ENERGY IS REALLY WHAT WE ARE SELLING.

Your audience, the people you serve, can get the "how" you do it from thousands of other people. Yes, there is nothing truly unique about your product or service—other than you. People want to spend time with you.

So, if that means buying your product or service to do just that—you can rest assured, they will.

This is one reason why tapping into your SOULFIRE and DIVINE PARTNERSHIP is so important. Although lots of people are friendly at work, few radiate joy, happiness, or peace. When you are in the flow of your SOULFIRE and DIVINE PARTNERSHIP you will.

People will be naturally attracted to you because of the electromagnetic fields that your heart sends out. And your nonverbal communication, tone of voice, and body language will all resonate at the same energetic frequency that attracts your audience to you.

Yes, we are talking "moth to the flame" scenario here.

You will be undeniably attractive to your audience not because of what you have said, done, or will do for them. But simply because of your energy.

AND WITH ENERGY BEING ABLE TO TRAVEL AT 2,200 KILOMETERS PER SECOND—WHICH IS BASICALLY GOING AROUND THE WORLD IN A LITTLE OVER 18 SECONDS—YES, SUCCESS CAN TRULY COME IN AN INSTANT.

LEARN.

When you work and live from a place of your SOULFIRE and DIVINE PARTNERSHIP the value of your work is not in how it manifests. It is in the energy that your work brings to the world that holds the value.

DO.

Keep a running list of what, who, and how your energy gets drained throughout the day.

Does hearing the sound of receiving a text message make you feel anxious? Does getting an email from a particular client or your mother-in-law make you want to run away and become a server at a small diner in rural Montana where no one and no technology can find you?

Track it and then take action to protect your energy at all costs.

BELIEVE.

It isn't what you do that makes you wanted. It is the energy in which you do it.

BECOME.

Be selfish about how, with whom, and where you put your energy. It is your responsibility as the hands and feet in your DIVINE PARTNERSHIP to make sure that your energy is always bringing your A-game. Dump the friends, clients, and co-workers whose energetic drama is bringing you down. Selfishness about your energy is the key to your ultimate success.

CONNECT.

Find places and hobbies that allow you to ground your energy while renewing your soul. For example, walking barefoot in the grass for 20 minutes on a sunny day is an easy way to ground your energy and your biorhythms too. Best of all, it's free.

Chapter 32

PUT YOUR MIND ON YOUR MOTIVE AND YOUR MOTIVE ON YOUR MIND

MAY YOU ALWAYS REMEMBER YOU AND LIFE ARE LIKE A MULTIFACETED PRISM: BEAUTIFUL, AWE INSPIRING AND ONE.

How many times do you pick up your phone when you are waiting for that one special person to text or email you?

Often.

How many times do you find excuses to stay on a social media platform longer, spend a little more time replying to another person's text, writing notes, read books—basically doing anything to stay connected to the person you are desperately seeking to hear from?

Many of us are intuitively like this when it comes to rediscovering our SOULFIRE. As children we still have a Divine connection that hasn't been dammed up by the social stories and beliefs of The OTHERS.

But soon enough, limitations and doctrine begin to set in. You only find God in a church. He is only available on Sunday. You have to tell another flawed human being about your sins. And if you want your life devoted to a Divine connection you better become a priest, brother, pastor, or nun.

Yep, for the longest time I secretly wanted to be a nun as a child because I thought that was the only way to have a life with the Divine. (Can you tell I was raised Roman Catholic?)

From the social stories, societal pressures, and simple time passing and seemingly receiving no response—you stop seeking, waiting, and you eventually fall into line like the rest. You begin to think that your desire for more—a life with heart and true connection—is just another fairytale you were told. Just like no White Knight is coming to save you, there is no Divine greatness, partnership, or life for you.

THAT IS EXACTLY WHAT THE OTHERS WANT YOU TO THINK. THAT FAIRYTALES AND GOD GO HAND IN HAND. THAT BOTH ARE NOT POSSIBLE, NOT REAL, AND ARE NEVER GOING TO HAPPEN IN YOUR LIFE.

So, we accept antiquated rules to fill the Divine void you hold deep inside of you. Such rules as:

- A firm handshake means you are confident, professional, and can handle the weight of whatever stress comes your way.

- A true lady would never kiss on the lips on the first date. Let alone do anything else.

- Women's skirts can only be so high and tops so low if you want to be taken seriously in life.

- Corsets, silk, and lace are never items for a serious businesswoman to wear at work.

- Guys in pale pink, lavender, and paisley are just a little too soft for the real leadership positions in the company.

We accept these bastardizations of influence, nonverbal communication, and social protocol in place of the Divine connection we long for. Though we accept it, it isn't fulfilling. It doesn't truly fill the void. And in turn we long for the fairytale, we long for the Divine.

WE AREN'T LOOKING FOR RULES—WE ARE LOOKING FOR THE RELATIONSHIP WE FEEL WE LOST WHEN WE CAME TO THIS SIDE OF HEAVEN.

Just like in fairytales, the Divine speaks to a deep root of the human heart, mind, and soul. And unlike the fairytales, your Godly partner is waiting for you. He is ready to cheer you on, be your knight, and create the life and relationships your heart has always desired.

THE FIRST STEP TO DOING JUST THAT IS TO BELIEVE.

You must think it first, believe it next, and then live it. Connecting with the Divine is truly that simple.

And with all good relationships and partnerships, it takes time. You have to put forth effort. Realize you are going to fail and be willing to try again. You have to overcome the outside speculation and internal chatter that this is nuts, you are nuts, and that you are wasting your time.

YOUR MIND TRULY IS THE BATTLEFIELD AND YOU MUST BE DETERMINED THAT YOU WILL CONTROL IT, NOT THE OTHERS.

LEARN.

There is no substitute or fast hack to the DIVINE PARTNERSHIP your heart and mind seeks.

DO.

As you write out the intention for every action you take each day, go one step further and ask yourself, "How does this affect me and my DIVINE PARTNERSHIP?"

Is the act an antiquated or poor substitute to the deeper relationship you seek? Is it an act that brings life to your SOULFIRE and DIVINE PARTNERSHIP in this world?

When you understand not just "why" behind your action, but the Divine connection, too you are able to not just engage in every act in your day with purpose and passion, but you can also find personal fulfillment in an entirely new light.

BELIEVE.

Your mind is more powerful than you fully realize. Protect it at all cost.

BECOME.

When we step back and look at the beings we are, it's easy to see that we are very multifaceted on a biological level alone. Yet if we dare think to bring this multifaceted perspective into our relationships, our work, our careers, our lives—we are told how confusing that would be. The underlying message is that no one would understand who we are; people couldn't relate.

Become the multifaceted person that you truly are in every situation. Embrace the totality that is. And use the depths of who you are intelligently throughout every day of your life. People won't get confused by who you are and what you are about. They will actually find it refreshing and relatable because they, too are multifaceted.

CONNECT.

The best way to put this into action is with NERI. NERI shows you all the possibilities that are unique to your personality and then allows you to take intelligent action by bringing your multifaceted self to all that you do.

Chapter 33

WORDS, WORK, WORTH, AND WEALTH

MAY YOU ALWAYS REMEMBER THAT YOU ARE NEVER ALONE.

Because we are so goal oriented, work oriented, and outcome driven—many of us have to reverse think and feel our way into our DIVINE PARTNERSHIP. By doing so, we stay connected to the truth of our purpose and true work, as well as satisfy the ego side of our heads and hearts.

Of course, the end goal is to live a life solely focused on our SOULFIRE and DIVINE PARTNERSHIP, but this is a lifetime of a process to uplevel into our truest meaning. And let's be honest, the life of NEW NOTORIETY is pretty darn sexy.

A LIFE OF NEW NOTORIETY ISN'T WHAT GETS OTHER PEOPLE OFF WHEN IT COMES TO SUCCESS. IT IS ABOUT WHAT UNIQUELY GETS YOU OFF.

In turn a life of NEW NOTORIETY looks completely different to the outside world but feels like perfect alignment to the person.

Over the years I have seen lives and brands go from the struggle for success to being in the flow of NEW NOTORIETY.

- For some of my clients, a life of NEW NOTORIETY is having the ability to move across the country to a place they have always dreamed of and build a multi six-figure business in the process.

- One particular client has a team of full-time staffers, where she works less, has more fun and her once struggling $33k a year business is set to be a multi-million dollar one—in under six years. This is what a life of NEW NOTORIETY looks like to her.

- And for others, a life of NEW NOTORIETY is creating a worldwide movement that will forever change the trajectory of a new generation.

For me, a life of NEW NOTORIETY is being madly in love with every single project or person I put my hands on. To help people tap into their SOULFIRES, and guide them to build DIVINE PARTNERSHIPS, and develop massively profitable and beautiful brands along the way. To have everything rooted in Divinely ordained relationships with myself and others and the freedom to effortlessly travel the world, speaking, training, and loving life with my love by my side.

SETTING THE STAGE FOR SUCCESS.

By understanding what you really want out of a life of NEW NOTORIETY you can successfully focus on the end goal, this idealist life of NEW NOTORIETY—and reverse engineer our way to the DIVINE PARTNERSHIP.

THE KEY HERE IS TO NEVER BECOME OUT OF BALANCE BY WANTING THE LIFESTYLE MORE THAN YOUR LIFE'S WORK.

We are simply looking for some tangible road markers of what a successful life and career looks and feels like to you so that you can see visible progress. While always being open to the betterment that the Divine has in store.

BY DEVELOPING A PATTERN OF INTENTION, WE MINIMIZE THE MISSTEPS AND DISCONNECTION FROM OUR TRUEST WORK—OUR SOULFIRE.

When this pattern becomes our reality, we realize that all we are responsible for doing is to set the stage per se and then allow our partnership and life to unfold. Meaning: we do our best to prep, plan, and think things through, and then let the Divine take action. For us to help we must be open to how the work, worth, and wealth shows up.

THE TRUE POWER OF WORDS.

Words are so much more than ways to categorize the items and experiences we have in life. We know logically that words have power, but far too often we carelessly throw our words around not consciously comprehending the true intent of their meanings.

We say we are "sorry" for things that we have no control over. We call ourselves dumb, overweight, not bright, or slow. We use self-deprecating humor to protect ourselves in the moment, but we end up hurting ourselves in the long run.

We use these throw away words innocently enough, but the long-term and short-term damage they do to our biology, subconscious mind, and energy is—on many levels—unmeasurable.

WORDS HAVE POWER FOR THREE MAIN REASONS. THE VIBRATIONAL QUALITY THE SOUND OF THE WORD MAKES, THE EMOTIONAL WEIGHT IT CARRIES, AND THE HISTORIC ROOTS

THAT WORD ORIGINATES FROM. THIS ISN'T
JUST A SPIRITUAL BELIEF; IT IS SCIENTIFIC
TRUTH.

- The Quantum Physics studies by Nobel Prize winning physicist, Werner Heisenberg, states that everything is energy. That nothing is truly solid. Everything is merely atoms and cells, which resonate on the same energetic frequency. So, all that is around you is a direct reflection of the energy you bring, and all your words represent.

- In the early 1990's Japanese scientist, Masaru Emoto, conducted experiments on the crystalized structure of ice, based on the words spoken to each sample. Vials of purified water were perfectly frozen. Then a phrase was attached to and spoken over the vial. Within 24 hours the cell structures of the ice changed— based on what it was being told: "I love you," and "You are perfect." or "I hate you" and "You are dumb."

- Emoto, conducted another experiment with two mason jars—each filled with two cups of perfectly cooked white rice. One jar was labeled "Thank You." and the other was labeled "You're a fool." The jars were then placed into a classroom where for thirty days the children were asked to say to the jar the label placed on it. As well as to "send" the emotion that was labeled on the jar, too. At the end of 30 days, the mason jar labeled "Thank you" was still perfect rice. While the jar labeled "You're a fool" was a gelatinous, decomposing mess.

Often as Success Rebels, we don't want to label ourselves, our work, or what we do. In doing so we are trying to keep our creative freedom flowing, but we open ourselves for others to define us with a label of their choice.

To define or label people is part of our human nature. Our minds need to quickly categorize and organize the information it receives, and labels do that. So, even if we try to buck the biological ways of our brains, we lose, and our brains win.

A TITLE IS JUST A TITLE—UNTIL IT ISN'T.

Our struggle to define ourselves roots in the social stories The OTHERS have ingrained in us. On one hand we want a title, the degree, the letters behind our name because it means that we have "made it."

On the other hand, we don't want to be confined to a role, industry, or relationship status.

Whether you choose a title or not, one will be given. And just like the rice or ice didn't choose their labels—aka titles—they were given one, which affected them on a cellular level because the rest of the world believed what that label noted.

So, take back the power in the words spoken over you and the titles given to you. Choose the adjectives that are true for you and speak to the truth of your SOULFIRE and DIVINE PARTNERSHIP.

This is not about creating some cheesy line to follow the phrase, "Hi, My name is Bob and I am a......" But it is about choosing words that are rooted in the true transformation, emotion, and experience your SOULFIRE comes from.

As we seek our partner and purpose, and put into action our work, let us remove the ideas of industry, audience, schooling, or anything else.

LET THE WORK, WEALTH, AND WISDOM COMING FROM FROM YOUR CORE DIVINITY AND SOULFIRE CREATE A LIFE STIRRING AND WORLD CHANGING TRANSFORMATION, WHICH IS ROOTED IN THE DEEPEST EMOTION YOU FEEL THE WORLD NEEDS TO EXPERIENCE.

Let us choose the words spoken over us.

Let us choose the words spoken about us.

Let us choose the words spoken over our work.

Let us choose the words spoken about our Soulfire.

Let us choose the words spoken over our DIVINE PARTNERSHIP.

Let us choose the words spoken about our life of NEW NOTORIETY.

Let us choose the words used to define our Success Rebel soul.

LEARN.

Words don't just shape your mind. They shape your cells, actions, intentions, and future.

DO.

Choose today which words do and do not define what your life of NEW NOTORIETY, the relationships of your dream, and the success of your heart means to you. Then only allow the words on your "do" list to be used when discussing those topics.

BELIEVE.

Words and how you define the world define your wealth.

BECOME.

Become a truth talker. Share the possibilities, solutions, and goodness you see in the world.

CONNECT.

Connect your words with the world. Send notes of encouragement and a job well done to strangers you simply meet in passing. Pause and tell the ones you love how you truly feel about them and the potential you see in them.

I believe in doing this so much that I actually started a line of greeting cards called *Truth. Love. Letters*. They can be found at (http://truthloveletters.com) They include non-politically corrected, raw truths, which I have shared with clients, friends, and loves. They aren't just cards that make someone feel good. They are cards that can create cellular transformation. And how cool is that?!?!

Chapter 34

WHY NICE "GUYS" DON'T MATTER

MAY YOU FOREVER KNOW THE PURITY AND DIVINITY OF YOUR HEART.

From a young age, we are all taught to be nice.

Be nice to your brother.

Be nice to your friend.

Be nice and share your toys.

As a child, if you chose not to be nice, well, you were in for it. Being in trouble with Mom or Dad, losing your favorite toy, having to miss out on your favorite event, or something far worse. Niceness quickly became your mark of acceptance and love.

The two foundational biological and social triggers we all instinctively crave.

NICE IS SO OVERRATED.

Soon enough though, you realize that being the nice guy kind of sucks. You don't get to do what you want, or when you want to.

So many children learn to appear nice to their parents, teachers, and The OTHERS, but actually manipulate, bully, and domineer those they can, getting their way and revenge for when they can't truly have their way. As we all know this relationship style is rarely grown out of as adults. It just evolves into manipulated, codependent and unhealthy relationships. But damn do you still appear to be a nice "guy."

Trust me this manipulated, codependent, narcissistic relationship style doesn't stop at your family's door. It affects your business relationships, reach and growth.

I have had many luxury branding clients fit this bill because money doesn't buy relational intelligence.

Let me tell you about one client who overall appeared to be an amazing person—until he didn't get his way. He wanted a hands-off approach where everyone did the work for him; unfortunately, he didn't have the money to pay for this luxury.

He tried to play the team against each other, play dumb so people would come to his rescue, and remind us all how much he loved his all-female team. Yes, we were amazing at what we did, but his subconscious intentions felt more domineering than do-good.

I need you to know the most frustrating thing. His brand is amazing. Truly could be a legacy brand. But it is this "false" nice demeanor, which he brought to the project that became a wild card when it came to the brand's success.

The lesson? Appearances can be deceiving, but nonverbal communication always tells the truth. Your body, face, and tone can't lie. And though you can work with a speech coach to correct your tone, and you can work with an impression manager or non-verbal communication coach to correct your body language from sharing your hearts intent— your face always tells your truth.

ARE YOU VENEER OR SOLID?

Social appearances won't get you far when it comes to success because they are just that, appearances.

AS MY GRANDMOTHER ALWAYS SAID, "NOTHING IS WORSE THAN PEOPLE FINDING OUT YOUR PERSONALITY IS VENEER."

If you have had a veneered piece of furniture in your home, then you know what that means. You can't sand it or refinish it. You can't nick it, scratch it, ding it, or scuff it because that flaw will always be seen. And you definitely can't spill a drink or something caustic like nail polish remover on it. The piece will never be the same. It can never be fixed.

Trust me I know this firsthand. I accidently spilled nail polish remover on a vanity table in the sixth grade and I still hear about how I ruined it! Plus, I am reminded of that mistake every time I go over to my Dad's house; I really did ruin the look of the table.

TO BE "FAKE NICE" OR NOT.

These are the same reasons why being fake nice won't work when it comes to living a life of success and NEW NOTORIETY. If you are being fake nice you will be found out. The OTHERS are hoping for it. Because if you are found out you will either run away in shame or everyone will know you are a fraud. Either way you won't pass the test of those checking you out—aka the wisdom and wealth in your weird. And that is all that matters to The OTHERS.

Fake nice or not, most truly successful people aren't known for their pleasant and hospitable personalities. Going against the social norms, going against The OTHERS, and rebelling against centuries of social engrainment requires a lot of cahoonas, strength, and personal fortitude. They simply don't equal the go with the flow "nice."

Here is the other thing about being "nice." That is an adjective that others bestow on you. It is purely subjective. You have no control over when, how, where, or for what it is used. When you seek such words to define yourself, The OTHERS win because they will never give you what you seek for long.

TO BE A TRUE SUCCESS AND SUCCESS REBEL FOR THAT MATTER, YOU MUST BE CRYSTAL CLEAR ON YOUR MOTIVES AT ALL TIMES AND NOT SEEK APPROVAL-BASED WORDS OR REACTIONS. YOUR INTENTIONS AND ACTIONS NEED TO BE THE RUTTER THAT MOVES YOUR WORK, SUCCESS, INFLUENCE, AND LIFE OF NEW NOTORIETY FORWARD—NOT THE PERCEPTION OF OTHERS.

LEARN.
Trying to be anything other than your true self is pointless.

DO.
Invest in knowing your true intentions and proactively modify any behaviors, which are not in line with your SOULFIRE, DIVINE PARTNERSHIP, and life of NEW NOTORIETY.

BELIEVE.
The real you is valuable, wanted, needed, and loved.

BECOME.
Become an investigator of the habitual actions, behaviors, and relationships you create. Look for patterns that no longer serve where your life is going and course correct either your reaction, situation, or the people involved.

CONNECT.
Discovering behavioral patterns that are no longer serving us can be a challenge because these patterns show up in your adult life, careers, and aspirations differently than when you were a kid.

Some of these learned behaviors are due to childhood trauma and others are just familiar behaviors that continue from generation to generation.

One of the easiest ways to break the root of these mindsets is to change the nonverbal communication that goes along with the habit.

The Success Rebel Academy, in conjunction with the International Society of Intelligent Influence has mini courses available, which will help you overcome some of those "nice" nonverbal behaviors you put on when you really should be taking it all off; being authentic.

Chapter 35

WHY EVERYONE MUST HAVE "IT"

MAY YOU ALWAYS REMEMBER THAT NO MATTER HOW FAR YOU HAVE COME, YOU ARE CAPABLE OF SO MUCH MORE.

We have all heard that success doesn't happen by accident. It's true. But many people take this line of thought as the "Do more. Be more. To get more." philosophy.

Society teaches us that more is always the answer. If you don't have enough money, go out and get more. Need better relationships, connections, or support—just go out and get more. Not having the level of respect, success, or influence you want—you simply need more.

THE IDEA OF MORE KEEPS US ALWAYS SEARCHING, ALWAYS WANTING, AND NEVER FEELING LIKE WHAT YOU HAVE IS ENOUGH. BUT MORE ISN'T THE ANSWER.

Searching for more of the same type of relationships, the same types of clients, the same streams of income will get you the same.

Same isn't going to make you a success.

Same feels good.

Same keeps you doing.

Same makes you seem important.

THE SAME IS SECRETLY GETTING YOU STUCK.

Same makes you a big fish in a little pond. Going after the same never allows you to know or grow to your full potential.

SAME IS DESIGNED TO WEAR YOU OUT AND BE OK WITH THE RESULTS AT HAND. SAME DOES NOT GET YOU TO SUCCESS.

True success, success on your terms, your way, rooted in your SOULFIRE isn't about more or same.

Working and succeeding in your DIVINE PARTNERSHIP is about dedication to the defined roles that are yours.

SUCCESS HAPPENS WHEN EVERYONE HAS THEIR ROLES IN WHICH THEY PERFECTLY EXECUTE.

The dessert chef doesn't decide to be the sommelier—and vice versa.

TEAMWORK IS SUPPOSED TO MAKE THE DREAM WORK.

If you truly want to take your SOULFIRE and DIVINE PARTNERSHIP and create a worldwide reach through a brand, business, or nonprofit you will need a team of people who can be the hands and feet of the mission alongside of you.

Now this all sounds well and good until you take action. Over my career I have built a luxury branding agency, production house, network studio, and publishing company. All of this required teams of people all doing their specific roles yet understanding the bigger picture at play.

What I have learned is that though we secretly hope to build a team that becomes the best pseudo family, who always gets along, understands each other and never really fights—that is only possible on the cast of *Friends*. What is more a reality is:

- That people get jealous and their egos rise,
- What once made them happy doesn't continue,
- Love makes people do stupid, stupid things.
- Those relational quirks they used to be able to hide—they can't anymore.
- Obsessions with the scope of various roles begins to blind staffers to the big picture you are building.
- As a Success Rebel and leader, you have to learn how to navigate what is best for your SOULFIRE, the work, your DIVINE PARTNERSHIP, and the life of NEW NOTORIETY that you are building. The failure to manage a team keeps bad relationships around, limits your scope, or deals with ego drama; all ways The OTHERS try to kill your work.

Because yes, ideally it would be nice to only hire people who see the world the way you do, it takes time for this truth—the authenticity—to show up.

WIN YOUR RACE—YOUR WAY.

Now this is not the one horse, one rider, one lane mentality. No, because arbitrary and limiting rule-following doesn't work either. To get to the next level of success, to break free of the proverbial mud you are currently stuck in, does require you to be intentionally tenacious every single day— to the roles, intention, and pursuit of your SOULFIRE.

Intentional Tenacity, aka IT, means that there will be some days where you simply don't feel like it. Some days where you would like to play smaller, not deliver excellence, or go rogue and cross over from the hands and feet work you are meant to do into something more posh, cool, or glory receiving.

I always tell my private branding clients that you know that you have the right brand for you when it passes the Worst Day Test. The Worst Day Test is when your life goes to absolute hell—when every fear, problem, relationship, money issue appears at the exact same time and all you want to do is hide.

- Will the roles that you are directly related to in your work every day have you show up?

- Do you love your customers so much that no matter if your life is falling apart you will happily serve them?

- When it looks like all is failing and your life is burning down around you, would it make you happy to go to work?

Being intentionally tenacious, being IT, requires a dedication to the end goal, as well as an abandonment of how others will perceive you. Because to the outside world you will look radical, intense, and utterly selfish. But they don't know and won't ever fully understand the intentions behind your actions. So, don't waste time trying to explain it. That in and of itself is a trap delivered by The OTHERS.

STAY FOCUSED, STAY CLEAR, AND STAY
INTENTIONALLY TENACIOUS ABOUT THE WORK
YOUR DIVINE PARTNERSHIP IS CREATING.

LEARN.

Being a Success Rebel means that you are a leader of your work, the people in your life, and the people who help bring your SOULFIRE to even more people than you could alone.

DO.

Be fearless in when and where you show up because your SOULFIRE and life of NEW NOTORIETY isn't about you or for you. It is about the ones you serve.

BELIEVE.

I am a leader.

BECOME.

Leadership is a skill you may have to struggle with initially because you aren't really sure how to do it. From social stories, to poor role models, to no models—ask your DIVINE PARTNERSHIP to show what leadership looks and feels like for you.

CONNECT.

Leadership is a skill and an art because in the end it is a relationship. Find leaders whom you love, learn what they do and why they do it. Use your NERI profile to try on leadership styles that fit your unique profile and see what works for you today— both with where you currently are and where you want to go.

Chapter 36

WHY BEING FAILURE OBSESSED CREATES MORE FAILURE

MAY YOU ALWAYS KNOW YOU ARE CAPABLE OF ANYTHING IF YOU KEEP YOUR MIND CLEAR AND YOUR HEART PURE.

Ask a success driven person what the number one thing is, which they don't want to be or experience in this life and they will tell you, "a failure." From a young age, The OTHERS have hijacked what falling and failure means to us.

FAILURE—THE FINAL FRONTIER.

When we are little kids just learning to walk, if we fall our parents rush to us and ask if we are ok. We learn quickly that falling can hurt us. Our primal biological instinct kicks in to remind us that falling could equal our demise.

We move forward into grade school and receiving an "F" is frowned upon because you aren't achieving, succeeding, or keeping up with the rest of the class. Therefore, you aren't smart enough, let alone successful in this subject.

The negative perception that we are taught to have around the idea of falling and failure creates fear, a mental/emotional frenzy, and full on disdain for any hint of the "f" word in our lives. This is exactly what The OTHERS want.

The risk of biological death or injury, not just social shame, is tied to failure. We refuse to face the gift it can be. With this blatant denial of any type of failure in our lives make us either play small so as to not experience great loss. Or we deny the gift of what not succeeding in the manner of which we initially thought can bring to us.

Failure isn't the opposite of success.

FAILURE IS SIMPLY A MISCALCULATION OF THE PROJECTED OUTCOME.

That's it. But before we realize that we miscalculated, there is faith.

FAITH AND FAILURE.

We have faith in the work that we are doing. We have faith in the positive, beneficial, and life changing results this work will create for us and for others. We have faith that we are in alignment with our SOULFIRE and DIVINE PARTNERSHIP.

FAITH IS AT THE HEART OF EVERY "FAILURE."

We have been trained to view failure as not hitting the bullseye perfectly. If you are a little high or a little low—you fail. The OTHERS have set the social story of chronic failure up because life on this side of Heaven is only fallible. Few things go according to plan. And it is our ability to course correct and continue that makes leaders succeed.

Think about it, with today's hyper focused viewpoint on failure:

- Christopher Columbus would be a failure because he didn't discover a shorter route to India.

- Thomas Edison would be a failure because it took him over 1,000 attempts before he made the first working light bulb.

- Plato would be a failure because many of his philosophies have now been debunked.

- John F Kennedy would be a failure because the United States didn't make it to the moon in his lifetime.

- Oprah would be a failure because she was fired from a job.

WHEN WE IRRATIONALLY DENY OR LIMIT OUR ACTIONS DUE TO POTENTIAL FAILING, WE LIMIT OUR FAITH ON THE POSSIBILITIES OF WHAT WE CAN ACHIEVE.

Instead of walking confidently to achieving the next road marker dreams on our life's path, we hobble ourselves from receiving the success we truly seek. Simply because we don't embrace the faith that is at the heart of every single thing that we do.

As with most tactics The OTHERS use, we get so distracted, and in fear of failure, that we don't see our faith eroding in front of us. Faith is what creates success. Faith is what will take your consistent work, dedication, and intentional tenacity and ultimately turn what seems like no results into life changing influence, grace, favor, and the life of NEW NOTORIETY you seek.

Focus on your faith.

LEARN.

Focus on the faith in your actions and learn from the results your faith produces.

DO.

Stop focusing on the specificity of the deliverable and start to focus on the intention behind it. Use the Soul Targeting method to help broaden your scope of what success looks, feels, and is to you. Don't forget your free digital copy of the *Success Rebel Go Guide*. This Soul Target resource is available at http://SuccessRebelBook.com.

BELIEVE.

Faith is what creates success.

BECOME.

If you have taken action on the prompts woven throughout this book, you are already a person who sees solutions around you. Let's take that one step further and become the person who sees the potential around you.

The potential in people.

The potential of your work.

The potential in your family.

The potential in your relationships.

The potential in what your DIVINE PARTNERSHIP can produce.

CONNECT.

Before you judge if your actions are a success or a failure pause and connect with the faith that started it all.

Chapter 37

HOW TO CREATE RELATIONSHIPS THAT WORK

MAY YOU ALWAYS KNOW THAT SUCCESS AND LIFE IS ROOTED IN RELATIONSHIPS WITH YOURSELF FIRST AND OTHERS SECOND.

"Relationships." I can feel the sigh of exhaustion coming out of you as you read that word.

For many of us, relationships feel overwhelming, tiresome, burdensome, and one sided. Few Success Rebels innately love to create and maintain relationships. Let's be honest, you would much rather do a hundred times more work than deal with an unfulfilling relationship. That is exactly how The OTHERS want you to feel.

M-O-O-O-VE OVER.

Just look at the world of online dating—where they turned the art of matchmaking into a cattle sale at the livestock barn. And that is exactly how people feel on those types of sites: scared, unloved, and desperate to not be overlooked. Because we all know what that means for the cattle and us—death.

Consider the possibility: they, the OTHERS, want you to find relationships hard, heavy, unfulfilling, hurtful, painful, and not worth the time or energy. The OTHERS want you to retreat into yourself vs. stepping into your SOULFIRE, and your DIVINE PARTNERSHIP, or to step out and fully connect with the humans you are meant to serve. They want you focused on the pain and the effort—not the outcome.

As you well know by now, distraction is one of the number one bad magic trick tactics The OTHERS use to keep us from being utterly selfish about our DIVINE PARTNERSHIP.

Look around at all of the social stories that tell us what is important on this side of Heaven: education, career, cars, kids. But these social stories and The OTHERS fail to show the common thread that actually does make such things important: relationships.

HUMAN OR NOT, SOUL LIVING CREATURES DESIRE RELATIONSHIPS.

To truly be healthy, thriving, and fulfilled, we need the connection, touch, and feeling that we are not alone in this world.

Animals get it, why not people?

- All of the female African elephants in a herd take care of all of the young.

- Orangutan moms hold onto their babies nonstop for the first four months of the little ones' lives.

- Female octopuses typically starve themselves to death as they protect their offspring.

As a whole the world is waking up to the root of what life is all about, and that is relationships.

LOVIN' HUMANITY HARD.

Let's be honest...most black sheep Success Rebels aren't the biggest fans of humanity at large. We don't want to create tons of relationships. We don't want everyone to know about our innermost thoughts, feelings, wants, and desires. And we don't have to.

We have been fed the lie that relationships have to be these deeply intimate, entangled experiences to be of any value. But they don't. Good relationships have healthy boundaries and limits. And we get to choose the boundaries and limits.

This doesn't make the soul to soul connection or experiences created together any less valuable. Such a relationship scope actually allows for success to occur because it isn't about creating a never ending, no holds barred, everything is on the table possibilities. By limiting the relationship possibilities, you create defined goals of achievement as well as space for additional relationships to occur.

But now we must go one step further and look at what makes relationships matter. The experiences.

This isn't a concept too far off as large companies like Groupon switched their marketing mentality away from the traditional "Do more. Have more. Be more." mindset and transitioned their message to creating more experiences.

Because success is our ultimate focus, and we are dedicated to our role of being the hands and feet in our DIVINE PARTNERSHIP and at the heart of it all is the experiences we create and the souls we create it with.

OUR SUCCESS TRULY COMES FROM THE EXPERIENCES WE CREATE WITHIN THE RELATIONSHIPS WE KEEP.

Now experiences don't have to be grand gestures or events. Yes, lavish weddings, going to beautiful places, and getting out of our daily lives can be amazing experiences. But no matter if you are looking large or small, great experiences are rooted in thoughtfulness.

GOOD BRANDS CREATE EXPERIENCES ALL THE TIME: CHRISTIAN LOUBOUTIN, MICHEL KORS, TARGET—AND YOU CAN TOO.

You will find that intention and attention are the key to great relationships and great success.

INTENTION sets the scope of the expectations and the energy for the moment while ATTENTION allows for whatever transpires to matter because it has significant meaning to the parties at hand. Great relationships and connections really are that easy.

Best of all being clear about the intention and paying attention to the needs of others is one of the great innate superpowers of many Success Rebels.

LEARN.

Everything in life is based on relationships.

DO.

Relationships are about creating a space of unconditional love. Take a moment and audit the relationships in your life. Do you need to be supported? Are you supporting the other person the way they need to be supported? Review your relationships individually and with the other party— with the intent to fulfill everyone's goals in ways that meet their love language and innate human needs.

BELIEVE.

Having outstanding relationships is totally possible for you in every area of your life.

BECOME.

Pause and consciously focus your intention and attention on the relationships that matter the most to you.

CONNECT.

Set monthly relationship goals for yourself. That can be how many new people you meet, connecting deeper with a friend, going to a networking event and having three coffee dates with people you meet...or going on a real date. By going out of your relationship comfort zone you get to know yourself better and learn how to use your NERI tools to connect with others more authentically and quicker too.

HOW TO STAY SUCCESS REBEL STRONG

Chapter 38

HOW TO OWN ANY ROOM WITHOUT EVER SAYING A WORD

MAY YOU ALWAYS KNOW THAT THE CHOICE TO INFLUENCE IS UP TO YOU.

The idea of being the CEO of your life is a very trendy one. But it is a misleading one if you truly want to be a Success Rebel and live a life of NEW NOTORIETY.

On many levels your life is your choice, your responsibility, your call. You can choose to stay in the status quo, or you can choose to change. It is all your baby. This CEO mindset also says that you are the smartest. You are in charge and you are the one calling the shots. So, what kind OF DIVINE PARTNERSHIP are you really working?

SUCCESS REBEL CEO.

We love the idea of the CEO because they own the room. But Success Rebel CEOs own their co-CEO status; they know they are the face of the business and in turn seek out marketing, media, and exposure opportunities for their SOULFIRE work. And when they ask for something, they usually get told "yes" because they just don't have human persuasion when it comes to owning the room, they have Divine influence, grace, and favor as well.

What is owning the room?

It is energy more than ego.

It is a presence, aura, and command.

It is an inspiration and curiosity raising wonderment.

It is an intensity, influence, and unexplainable desirability.

All without ever saying a word.

It is easy to get excited and get started with working your SOULFIRE, creating within your DIVINE PARTNERSHIP, and live the lifestyle with all the NEW NOTORIETY perks you have always wanted. Staying committed to the partnership can be the challenge.

Like going to the gym, if you stop your workout routine once the results start showing you eventually lose that which you gained; the same holds true with YOUR DIVINE PARTNERSHIP.

DIVINE PARTNERSHIP or not, it is still a partnership. You may not physically sit across from your partner; the type of relationship is the same. It is about mutual respect, appreciation, agreement, and working towards the same goal. And though you most likely won't receive audible replies to your agreements, the internal knowing is there.

Like with an earthly partner, it is your responsibility to stay in shape on all levels so that you can deliver your side of the agreement at the highest caliber possible. And though this makes logical sense, most of us would rather "do and be done" than complete the kind of work to show up at our highest level.

This is exactly how people fail. How people sabotage themselves, their success, their dreams, and the life of NEW NOTORIETY they seek.

SELF TO SERVE.

The reason why Success Rebels have to be selfish is because you have to take care of you first. Yes, it is the whole put your own oxygen mask on first scenario.

BECAUSE WE ARE THE HANDS AND FEET IN THIS
DIVINE RELATIONSHIP IT IS EASY TO GET OUR
MINDSET AND VALUE SKEWED INTO THINKING
THAT OUR ACTIONS MATTER MORE THAN US.

But when we show up from an overworked,
exhausted, underappreciated, mentally and
emotionally raw place we don't just fail to make a
good impression, we fail to read the true clues and
properly discern the true motives and underlying
stories of The OTHERS that are at play. Being the
hands and feet of the partnership is about so much
more than just doing the work.

You are the face of the relationship. It is your
nonverbal communication, energy, and body
language that people pick up on. You are the one
who will be able to positively influence the situation
or not.

OF COURSE, YOU ARE WALKING INTO ANY
SITUATION WITH DIVINE GRACE, BUT IN THE
END YOU ARE THE ONE CLOSING THE DEAL.

INTELLIGENT INFLUENCE.

This is why you must be intelligent about who you
influence and how you do it. Influencing just
anybody won't work when you are ready to create
intentional relationships. And then, you must be

prepared to use to your advantage the 50,000 plus impressions the average modern businessperson makes online and offline.

Let's put that into a clear perspective. Back in the 1970's the average business professional made 50,000 impressions in one month. They made a combined total of 50,000 handshakes, phone calls, meetings, networking events, business card passes.

TODAY THE AVERAGE BUSINESS PROFESSIONAL WHO IS ON SOCIAL MEDIA FOR PERSONAL AND BUSINESS MAKES 50,000 IMPRESSIONS IN ONE DAY.

I would imagine that it was hard enough in the 1970's to remember how you came across in all of those 50,000 instances. In today's society it is darn impossible unless you know how to always make sure the best version of you is showing up. Be it the woman you just met in line waiting for the bathroom four minutes ago, that social media post from four months ago, an old speaker one-sheet page still online from 4 years ago, or that high school photo a friend just tagged you in that is roughly 40 years old—you are always making an impression. And these impressions add up to what people think of you and how people feel about you.

If you use the art of INTELLIGENT INFLUENCE these 50k+ impressions can be to your advantage. By understanding the when, where, and how you are coming across you can easily take the vast array of how and where you are being seen—and use it to the advantage of your SOULFIRE, DIVINE PARTNERSHIP, and life of NEW NOTORIETY.

Best of all it all starts with your intentions. Your intentions help set your energy, the electro-magnetic fields your heart gives off, clarify your nonverbal communication, body language, tone of voice and even your choice in words. But to be really clear about your intentions you have to have proper rest, nourishment, and appreciation for your body, mind and spirit.

Oh, but, it truly is that simple! Because it is so simple it is a challenge to set aside and shut off all of the voices of The OTHERS and the social stories they bring. So instead of showing up as the best version of ourselves we sabotage the impressions we make by questioning our every move vs. being in the moment.

After working with entrepreneurs for decades, INTELLIGENT INFLUENCE and impression management is what works when you want to come across as the unapologetic powerhouse and success rebel that you are—or seek to be.

7 FIGURE SIGNALS.

I have coached and trained hundreds of people on how to overcome their fears and use the impressions they make to their advantage. Whether it is asking investors to buy into your vision or meeting the parents of your love for the first time,

I've discovered there are numerous unique signals that can have you owning any room and any situation no matter how you feel. I call these signals the 7 FIGURE SIGNALS because they truly help turn any situation into 7-figure earnings.

Wouldn't you love to:

- Show up and shine as a true expert

- Come across as a leader

- Be viewed as a handler—aka the one who has everything under control

- Close the deal anywhere, anytime

- Get to the truth of any situation fast

- Create an experience of community, connection, and collaboration

- Always appear fearless

- Be viewed as a visionary

- Negotiate any disagreement

- Handle small talk and that 30 second pitch

- Come across as confident, even if you don't feel like it

But for INTELLIGENT INFLUENCE, 7 FIGURE SIGNALS, or just in general making a good impression happen, you must show up as the best version of you. So put your preferable oxygen mask on daily before you try to be of service to others.

LEARN.
The impressions you make equal the influence and income you create.

DO.
You can never consciously and strategically manage 50,000+ impressions a day even if you had the personal handlers of the Kardashians. The best way to make sure you are making the most out of these 50,000 daily opportunities is by always showing up as the BEST VERSION OF YOU.

I have included some of my favorite BVY exercises in the *Success Rebel Go Guide* (http://successrebelbook.com) but you can check out loads of BVY vlogs on the International Society of Intelligent Influence's website (https://www.impression.management/)

BELIEVE.
Self + Service = Success.

BECOME
By being a person of intention first and action second, you create an unspoken presence and desirability of who you are and what you are about.

CONNECT.
Learn how to master the 7 FIGURE SIGNALS, INTELLIGENT INFLUENCE, and Owning Any Room; it is part art and part science. We have an ever-growing list of mini courses on these topics all designed to give you bite size information in which you can take action and see results fast available at the Success Rebel Academy, at: (http://successrebelacademy.com)

Chapter 39

WILL THE REAL YOU PLEASE STAND UP?

MAY YOU KNOW THAT THE REAL YOU IS THE ONLY VERSION OF YOU THAT THIS WORLD NEEDS.

The first step to leaving any cult is to recognize the lies within their teachings. Breaking free from The OTHERS and the social stories you were raised with is very much like leaving a cult. The first step of realization seems like the hardest, until you realize you no longer know yourself.

Now I have never been in a cult, but I have been in a dysfunctional marriage. So...pretty damn similar. Nearly nine years after the marriage ended, I still realize that the guilt or judgement I feel in a particular situation has nothing to do with me, my intention or my worth. But it has everything to do with how my now ex would perceive the social situation and would want me to comply with the ways and expectations of The OTHERS.

Cult or not. Bad relationship or not. None of us have achieved adulthood without having some type of social programming burned into our psyche. Many of us have our shit together for the most part. At least we like to think so. And if you want proof on how awesome you are, all you have to do is turn on the television and look at almost any reality tv show and realize you aren't that bad off. But self-diagnosing that you are just A-Okay is exactly what The OTHERS want you to do.

BOMBS AWAY.

Self-sabotaging behavior comes in so many forms. From choosing the same type of romantic partner over and over again to creating financial drama for yourself even when logically you know better. The travesty lies in the fact that this is all simply because of your subconscious mind.

> By not digging deep and consciously choosing how you want to show up in various life situations, you allow subconscious programming to take over.

> By not choosing how you want to show up, all of those sabotaging, fear based, ticking time bombs from The OTHERS simply lie in wait.

These are where NERI comes in.

Neuro Emotional Relationship Intelligence, NERI, is more than just a personality profile. It reveals your potential and how you can authentically choose different relationship patterns, reactions, or responses to life by knowing all that you are capable of.

Think if it this way. When you were born into this world and came on this side of Heaven, the world was your oyster. There were so many possibilities of how you could show up, what you could do and with whom. But then, life's experiences, social stories, and The OTHERS began having you choose one way of being and doing over another. Both authentically you, one version served you better in the moment. The problem is those moments became your memory. And in turn the way you habitually began to act or react to any given situation in life—rather than making conscious choices.

THE PROBLEM IS THE MOMENT BECAME YOUR MEMORY. AND IN TURN THE WAY YOU HABITUALLY BEGAN TO ACT OR REACT TO ANY GIVEN SITUATION IN LIFE.

NERI isn't about judgment or limitations. NERI is about understanding your true self so you can break limiting patterns in a way that is in alignment with your true self and understand others so that you can create authentic, powerful, passionate, and fulfilling connections from the beginning with ANYONE.

NERI allows you to naturally lead with the right foot when meeting a new business contact. You can instinctually know exactly what relationship style, expectation, and organizational structure works for you and what is automatically expected by others.

NERi allows you to understand who you truly are on profound and practical levels. Like giving you authentic insights into your:

- Relationships
- Priorities
- Workflow
- Success
- Organizational perspective
- Personal style
- Mindset
- Stress, problem-solving, and self-sabotage habits

And because life is about relationships, NERi isn't just about having a better relationship and life with yourself. It is about having dynamic relationships with others too. NERI allows you to:

- Know how to instinctively connect with anyone, anywhere in an authentic and honest manner for both of you.
- Understand the unspoken expectations and habits of the other party so that such innate traits don't sabotage the relationship or project.

- Instantly know what matters to a person you have never met. Allowing you to curate your message (or sales pitch) in a way that speaks to that persons' true desire first.

- Gain powerful insights into your clients, co-workers, companions, and kiddos, so you create more engaging relationship moments (because you now know how to authentically relate even in the most frustrating times.)

Understand yourself, overcome your sabotaging habits, which you know hold you back, create better relationships, and use your nature to your life's and work's advantage—what is more fun than that?!?!

NOTHING!!! (at least I don't think so.)

The only way for you to grow past your habits and past the social stories is to fully understand who you are and begin to consciously choose how you show up. Engaging in the art of choice is intentional. It helps call forth and bring together all of the energetic and physical pieces of the work you are doing.

CHOOSING EMPOWERS YOU TO NO LONGER BE THE VICTIM OR INNOCENT BYSTANDER.

You are a full-fledged leader showing up in your DIVINE PARTNERSHIP with nothing holding you back.

When you show up as the leader, in all your Success Rebel ways, so does the Divine.

The idea that "like attracts like" is more than some human psychobabble. It is an energetic, spiritual, and success principle as well. Showing up as the best version of you, uninfluenced by THE OTHERS is an attractor; you can attract the same in your life of NEW NOTORIETY as well.

LEARN.

Habits don't have to keep holding you back. You can choose to authentically change any habits likely to sabotage your success.

DO.

Understanding who you are and are not isn't being selfish, or prideful, nor does it fit any other social story The OTHERS want to throw your way. When you understand your true self, you begin to make choices that empower your work, relationship, and lifestyles.

BELIEVE.

Never forget that the real you are really worth knowing.

BECOME.

Be the person that people want to have relationships with; have genuine, honest, no alternative motive relationships with them first.

CONNECT.

Personally, I find that learning about NERI is best done in a small group because you are able to understand yourself and see the other options of who you could choose to be modeled in front of you. I personally lead two NERI small groups a year. You can get more details on that and NERI overall at (http://neri.io).

Chapter 40

ENERGY. INSTINCT. ENVIRONMENT.

MAY YOU NEVER GET IN YOUR OWN WAY.

Lifestyle protocols have always been social norms. Where we live, how we live, with whom we live have always been influenced by others more than by our choices. Yet, if succeeding in life is a rebellious act, then how you live life must follow as well.

Being successful, having influence, grace, favor, and living a life of NEW NOTORIETY aren't tasks you check off your "to do" list. These aren't one and done items to complete.

BEING A SUCCESS REBEL IS A MINDSET AND WAY OF LIFE.

Because of this reality, an average approach to life simply won't do.

Now, that doesn't mean we are going to the extreme of champagne wishes and caviar dreams. Living a life of NEW NOTORIETY isn't necessarily about luxury or excess. A life of NEW NOTORIETY does come with perks per se. It is the payout for your DIVINE PARTNERSHIP. That could be a nice house, great relationships, going on nice trips. Whatever your dreams are, that is the life of NEW NOTORIETY you will receive. This lifestyle will organically support you, your SOULFIRE, and DIVINE PARTNERSHIP.

But while you are getting "there," and even once you "arrive," you need to focus on three key areas that can quickly sabotage your mindset and in turn work at large: energy, instinct, and environment.

ENERGY.

We have already covered that your energy and your income are tied together closely.

How you energetically show up matters. Many Success Rebels have empathic tendencies which means they can feel the emotions of the people they are dealing with. So even if you control the people in your physical space, do you regulate the people in your online spaces? Most likely not, but their energies still affect you.

In addition to people, you can recognize how much the technology, lightbulbs, and appliances we surround ourselves with can disrupt our energetic frequencies and make it more challenging for us to show up fully.

- There are special cell phone cases and laptop mats that can be used to minimize the radiation exposure when using such items.

- Because we sleep with so many electronic devices around our beds there are now Grounding sheets that help nullify the radiation and electrical currents that are interfering with your body's natural electrical current.

- Though there is no scientific proof, Hinduism and Buddhism have taught about the grounding, protective, and clearing nature that certain crystals and stones can have on the chakra system.

ENERGY IS EVERYWHERE AND IT IS OUR RESPONSIBILITY TO USE IT TO OUR ADVANTAGE.

INSTINCT.

The OTHERS love to discount our innate instinct. More than just our primal subconscious mind, our biology remembers. Many of us do not fight off real life mountain lions every day, so being able to "read" people and listen to their real truths intuitively is a genuine gift.

Methods like INTELLIGENT INFLUENCE and NERI can help you reconnect with this primal side, but there are others like meditation that help equally well. Studies find that people who successfully meditate for ten minutes or more on a daily basis, have a greater connection between their two brain hemispheres, which makes it easier to read, process, and respond to nonverbal cues.

And if you are by chance a lady Success Rebel, you already have a leg up on the boys. As the rush of testosterone in utero, it also transforms an embryo into a male fetus also naturally separates the two hemispheres of the brain. Therefore, your brain hemispheres are closer together and you can communicate more effortlessly.

ENVIRONMENT.

The environment you surround yourself with matters on so many levels. The energetic logistics and people, but also the creative flow of the landscape, which can enhance or suppress your ability to positively produce.

Outside of vortexes, simply how the subcultural in a region runs will naturally affect how you behave. It is human nature and smart biology to mimic our surroundings. And even though society has "evolved" we still do it to this day.

This is one reason why I always bring my luxury branding clients to one of three cities to work: New York City, Las Vegas, or Palm Springs.

- New York City because of the fast pace, hustle energy, and the best of the best are there.

- Las Vegas because anything is possible. One hundred years ago, the Vegas strip didn't even exist. Men thought of it, built it, and look, people came.

- And lastly, Palm Springs, California, which I use when I sense my clients need to ground themselves, reconnect, and create in a revolutionary timeless manner.

By consciously using a city's cultural stories to your advantage you can expedite your growth, influence, and your ability to authentically expand as you choose new ways to react with your NERI profile in mind.

Being a successful Success Rebel is knowing when and how to use your biology, social stories, and subconscious triggers to your advantage.

ACCEPTING THE STATUS QUO IN ANYTHING WILL LIMIT YOUR ABILITY TO INFLUENCE, GROW, AND SUCCEED IN THE MANNER THAT IS POSSIBLE.

It doesn't mean you have to reject all of society, but as with every action you take, it is about consciously choosing your actions and reactions vs. falling into the habitual stories of The OTHERS.

LEARN.

You can use your biology, subconscious triggers, and social stories to your advantage.

DO.

Begin to take back your control by using your energy, instinct, and environments to your advantage. Begin to take notice of where and when you think clearly, have more energy, more creativity, feel happier, and where you are more in love, more connected with yourself and others. Then take that information and begin to discern "why." Once you know that repeat, repeat, repeat.

BELIEVE.

You are more powerful than you know.

BECOME.

Begin to plan the important stuff of life, work, and your SOULFIRE around the places and times when you are primed for success. Meaning: if you need to have an important heart to heart conversation and you are calmer in the afternoon taking a walk, set your conversation up for success by having it in the afternoon on one of those walks.

CONNECT.

We have been taught from an early age not to connect with our biological and energetic sides. Begin to explore what works for you; go forth with an investigator mindset and explore what works in your best interest—not necessarily everyone else.

Chapter 41

HOW WINNING MARIO BROTHERS MAKES YOU A WINNER IN LIFE

MAY YOU FULLY LIVE YOUR SOUL'S DESIRES.

Success is a funny thing. It is never what is expected on many levels. A lot of people talk about success as the uphill battle as if you are mountain climbing to the top. But I have never personally experienced or seen such a linear climb.

From my experience, success normally shows up like a game of Mario Brothers. Where you think you are going after your goal only to fall into a pit with crocodiles. And as with everything, you have to reprogram your thinking that the crocs are bad.

After all it is only a social story and the energy you bring that makes this seeming set back have power.

In *Mario Brothers* games the crocs don't show up because you are failing. You are actually gaining and winning in the game. They show up to see if they can mentally get you off your winning streak. The same holds true in life!

CALM ILLUSION.

I like to call it the Calm Illusion. I find with my branding clients no matter how much I prep them on how a product launch goes or a relaunch will transpire, everyone always thinks theirs will be perfect. In such instances it is rarely the tech or execution that creates the drama, it is normally a client's fear that shows up front and center.

Recently I had a new neighbor move into the house next door. These neighbors have three large dogs that bark all the time. One afternoon I was outside in the yard watching my kittos explore when the dogs started barking, and barking, and barking.

Then all of sudden that dog was sitting on top of the six and a half foot-tall brick wall that divides my yard from the neighbors. After yelling at the dog to get down, I went to tell the neighbor what had happened and suggested she may need to be aware her dog is capable of doing such a thing.

The wife could have cared less and said that she had trained her dogs to be "killers." And if anything were to happen it would be my fault. That is a Calm Illusion—or delusion in this case.

Yes, even in real life, everything can be going your way and then bam! Those clear pathways get messy with some croc illusions.

CROCS AREN'T ALL THAT BAD.

Like Mario Brothers, the crocs don't have to kill you. And in reality the fear that manifests as a lack of financial resources, an ex-love showing back up, a friend or coworker betraying you—all play into your greatest fears. But they don't hold real weight in harming you if you don't stop.

These fears, like those crocs, are trying to get you off your mental game. They are trying to see if you will break focus and stop going after your dreams. And like in Mario Brothers, if the crocs don't succeed there will be another enemy that will come your way. That is the game and that becomes the game of life when you choose success over illusions and the social stories of The OTHERS.

As the bombs are being hurdled your way, you must stay true to what you are and what your DIVINE PARTNERSHIP creates.

YOU MAY HAVE ONE SOULFIRE, BUT IT WILL MANIFEST ITSELF IN NUMEROUS WAYS.

Don't get scared off, shrink back, or follow a solo road simply because you feel the crocs are nipping at your feet.

You are not the one horse, one lane, one niche wonder that The OTHERS talk about. You are a Success Rebel.

SUCCESS REBELS ARE CHARIOT DRIVERS.

You have your SOULFIRE, your chariot, and all of your efforts, impressions, works, methods, outreaches are all going in one direction—toward the life of grace, favor, influence, and NEW NOTORIETY you desire.

YOU AREN'T SOLO SO YOU DON'T NEED TO CHOOSE A SOLO PATH.

You have a DIVINE PARTNERSHIP who has your back and is guiding you to your soul's true work.

DON'T LET THE ILLUSION OF LIFE STOP YOU FROM PLAYING ALL IN.

Learn.
It is your perspective that makes you a success or someone who simply settles.

Do.
Don't fall for the social story that you are so special that nothing bad will ever happen to you. Especially as you step out in a big way—know that opposition will come. And when it does don't look at it as a setback. Look at it as proof that you are on the right Soulfire path.

Believe.
Opposition is no obstacle.

Become.
Never forget that you run your own race. Don't be the person who gets lulled into believing the only way you can succeed is under The others' terms and timeframes.

Connect.
I can't stop saying it enough, find a community that works for you, even if it is a community of two. Being around like-minded, Success Rebels is the best way for you to succeed on your terms. And if the Success Rebel Society isn't for you, reach out to me at (http://alicraig.com) and we will see what we can do.

Chapter 42

INFLUENCE.
INTENTION.
INSPECTION.

MAY YOU ALWAYS KNOW HOW TRULY STRONG YOU ARE.

If you are looking for an easy life, let me spell it out for you: don't go after your dreams; don't live your SOULFIRE or work from a place of your DIVINE PARTNERSHIP. Living a life of NEW NOTORIETY looks glamorous but being a Success Rebel isn't for the faint of heart or people who want to sit on their laurels.

Being a Success Rebel requires a strong fortitude and intentional tenacity like few have, which hints to why few see their dreams fully become their reality. The beauty is that being a Success Rebel doesn't require some great physical strength or require you be a mental genius who can speak seven languages.

A Success Rebel is mentally strong. They audit their minds and emotions. Each is clear about intentions, understand how, when and who to influence, and always inspect the story at play.

A SUCCESS REBEL IS MENTALLY STRONG.

Because you see, The OTHERS have been at their games for centuries and they aren't stopping any time soon. One cannot assume that the revelations and assumptions, which occurred when you first began to break free from the cult of The OTHERS still holds true today.

The OTHERS are smart and cunning. They know how to use societal change to their advantage—not yours. And they can change the social story around a situation in a few short years, not generations.

Look at the social acceptance of tattoos for instance. In the 1980's tattoos were rarely seen. The majority of people who had them were of questionable pasts or a reminder of a drunken night out. Then the 90's hit and tattoos became trendy once again. Butterfly tramp stamps grace the lower backs of many a 40-year-old woman today. Fast forward another twenty years, and tattoos are socially acceptable in most industries and mainstream. Even showing your ink off at work is OK in many situations.

Why is that?

The OTHERS no longer found the suppression beneficial.

WE CAN NEVER GET SO FOCUSED IN BEING THE HANDS AND FEET TO OUR WORK THAT WE FORGET TO PAUSE AND INSPECT THE CURRENT CULTURAL CLIMATE OF THE PERCEIVED SOCIAL STORY AT PLAY.

As a Success Rebel it is our responsibility to exercise due diligence and understand the social game at play; to be strategic about how we use it to our DIVINE PARTNERSHIP advantage. Being blindly naive is a luxury we surrender when we choose to step forward and live the dreams of our souls on this side of Heaven.

LEARN.

Society is evolving at a faster pace than ever before. Where brands use to evolve their look and message every 4-6 years, we now see it happening every 4-6 months or sooner now. This means that the social stories you have grown up with may not have the same connotation or social bias as they did in the recent past.

DO.

Success Rebels are leaders and as a leader you need to take proactive measures to evaluate if there is a change in a social story that may affect how you present yourself, SOULFIRE to the world, or live a life of NEW NOTORIETY.

BELIEVE.

Your influence and intention are always your choice.

BECOME.

Be conscious about the ebbs and flows of your body. Being a powerful Success Rebel means you are a warrior. Take care of yourself on all levels so that you can never be taken advantage of.

CONNECT.

Recognize how the shifting social stories can be used to your advantage. By connecting with people in complementary fields where your audience crosses over, you are able to see potential shifts in your work early on, which allows you to be a true influencer at a higher level to your community.

Chapter 43

THE LIE THAT SOLO EQUALS SUCCESS

MAY YOU FOREVER KNOW THAT SUCCESS COMES TO THE COMMITTED FEW.

By now you realize that the social stories you have been taught are a whopping pack of stinky lies. Yet even though we know this, there is one social story that many Success Rebels struggle with. The lie that all great success happens solo.

Yes, we hear the cute expression, "Teamwork makes the dream work." But 9 times out of 10 the leading headline story is how a single mom went from welfare to six figures in a month. Or how a teenager built a multibillion-dollar business all alone in his parent's basement.

SOCIETY CELEBRATES SOLONESS.

That reality alone should be seen as a red flag to your Success Rebel mind, but for many of us it isn't. Our Divine partner is, well, Divine, and not visible. It is easy to fall for the mental trap that going solo will gain you success.

When a lioness hunts, she tries to get her prey alone and away from the pack. Alone the lioness knows that the animal is vulnerable and most likely will lose the fight. The OTHERS know this about you, too. This hints of the current cultural obsession with work from home, freelance, and solo entrepreneurship.

Don't fall for the trap.

Now that does not mean that you join any old group or go to any old meetup. You know controlling your energy is key to your success. So, choose wisely.

This is one reason why I created the Success Rebel Society. This online platform is a convenient place to stay focused, join live virtual trainings and make connections for in-person meetups as you see fit. I know first-hand how the right people can be powerful in propelling your dreams forward.

My hope is that the society welcomes all Success Rebels. The newbies to the game—and seniors like you and me. When you have a place that "gets" you and is dedicated to creating beneficial relationships and experiences for everyone to grow and succeed— magic happens.

But wherever you find community, find one that "gets" your heart, vision, and purpose. We all need a safe place to land—one that meets our human needs and inspires us to go after our SOULFIRE and live the lives of NEW NOTORIETY to which we are called.

LEARN.

Yes, going it alone will kill you and your ability to truly live your life of NEW NOTORIETY. But that does not mean you need a gaggle of followers either. Even one person who has your back and cheers you on is better than none. And hint, hint, you already have one—your Divine partner.

DO.

Find ways that connect that feel good to you.

BELIEVE.

No one person or thing can stop you with your Divine partner by your side.

BECOME.

Consciously break out of your shell and shy habitual ways by using your unique NERI profile, biology, environment, energy and subconscious mind to your advantage.

CONNECT.

Don't let The OTHERS fool you that you are alone or so "out there" that no one can understand. There are so many reasons that connection even on a small level is important for you, even if it is just to have the reassurance that what you think is false—is more powerful than you know.

Chapter 44

NEVER BACK DOWN

As this part of the Success Rebel story comes to a pause, I want you to know how fully capable you are.

Being a Success Rebel isn't an easy road and sometimes it feels more like you are on a cross country adventure being chased by zombies in the forest at night. But I honestly believe that you and I can do it.

Now you may be thinking that this is totally BS because I most likely haven't met you yet. But let me share one last thing with you.

You know my SOULFIRE roots in beauty and love, but the gift I have always had is the ability to sense the possibilities in people. I don't just see it. I can sense it!

It is what makes my branding and production work great.

It is what gives me insights into people so that I could birth NERI, NEURO HUMAN BRANDING, and Intelligence Influence.

And it is also what makes my belief in you true.

Because the person who has made it all the way through this book has a strong burning desire in themselves to have their lives matter.

They are unapologetic, fiercely loyal, and have more of a servant's heart than most people realize.

They aren't scared away from a fight or going solo, though that isn't what they would choose. They are Success Rebels through and through.

They are YOU!

I am so honored to have gotten to know your energy and you mine through these pages.

I look forward to the moment when we meet in person, Success Rebel to Success Rebel.

Love + Gratitude,

Ali

APPENDIX

RESOURCES

SUCCESS REBEL GO GUIDE.

I have loads of resources I created just for you and this book at http://SuccessRebelBook.com. Here you can grab your free digital copy of the *Success Rebel Go Guide.* The "Go Guide" has many of the exercises I talk about at the end of each chapter ready and waiting for you to go take action.

SUCCESS REBEL SOCIETY.

And because community, connection, and love are so important I highly encourage you to check out the online and real-world community my team and I run at http://successrebelsociety.com. I create a monthly area of focus for our society members to help excel personally and professionally by fully stepping into their badass selves.

From 21-day action plans to access to the mini-courses available at the Success Rebel Academy, and of course live office hours as well as meet ups around the world. My team and I strive to create the supportive environment that all Success Rebels need to excel. Use the code "I Am A Success Rebel" to get 10 free days in the society.

PODCAST NIRVANA.

If you love to listen and learn we have you covered. Head on over to Notoriety Network's (http://notorietynetwork.com) and check out all of the podcasts we have in store for you. Now these aren't your average podcasts. As with everything I do, I want to give you the most bank for your investment. Concise, to the point, and action oriented are what these podcasts are.

Pay special attention to the following:

- Success Rebel (well, duh!)
- The Human Element (all about NEURO HUMAN BRANDING)
- INTELLIGENT INFLUENCE CEO (all ABOUT INTELLIGENT INFLUENCE and Impression Management)
- Soulfire Life (all about living your SOULFIRE everyday)
- Meet NERI (all about the NERI profile method for yourself and relationships)

LIVING THE SUCCESS REBEL CEO LIFE.

It is one thing to live your SOULFIRE and life of NEW NOTORIETY in your everyday life. But when your DIVINE PARTNERSHIP leads you into a business, you aren't just upping your Success Rebel game. You are up leveling your vision, visibility, best version of you at hyper speed.

Our Success Rebel CEO intensive is an in-person training and multimedia platform designed to create social proof about your message, elevate your industry visibility, while leveraging your influence with your branding and marketing efforts as well as with national and international media outlets. Learn more about these in person intensives at http://successrebelceo.com

SUCCESS REBEL PLAYLIST.

Music doesn't just change moods and move bodies. It changes emotions and biology. Four things greatly needed to stay in your Success Rebel frame of mind. Here are a few of my go to tunes.

- For King and Country, *Burn The Ships*
- Katy Perry, *Fireworks*
- Bon Jovi, *Blaze of Glory*
- Garth Brooks, *The Dance*
- Michael Jackson, *Man In The Mirror*
- Marconi Union, *Weightless*
- Kelly Clarkson, *Stronger*
- Skillet, *Stars*
- Hillsong, *United. Oceans*
- Lady Gaga, *Born This Way*
- Lauren Daigle, *Rescue*
- Queen, *We Are The Champions*
- Mandisa, *Overcomer*
- Des Ree, *You Gotta Be*
- Eminem, *Not Afraid*
- Bon Jovi, It's My Life
- John Lennon, *Imagine*
- Christina Aguilera, *Beautiful*
- The Beatles, *All You Need Is Love*
- Gloria Gaynor, I Will Survive
- Kanye West, *Stronger*

SUCCESS REBEL MANIFESTO.

We believe that success is our destiny.

We believe that our life is no accident.

We believe that we all have a unique Divine purpose - aka a SOULFIRE.

We believe that our dreams are road makers on our life's path.

We believe we are the hands and feet in a greater DIVINE PARTNERSHIP.

We believe that relationships are rooted in with yourself first and others second.

And that your SOULFIRE is like art. People can imitate the master, but there is only one true master.

We believe that success comes from service.

We believe in shedding the mindset of political correctness.

We believe that people are born knowing love and learning fear.

We believe that everything can turn around in an instant.

We believe that energy creates income.

We believe that you can always choose again.

We believe that we are all growing into the true depths of our capabilities.

We believe that if we are on this side of Heaven there is more for us to do.

And that our intentions rule everything.

We believe that success doesn't happen solo.

We believe that consistency is king.

We believe that it is our duty to show a little more love in everything we do.

We believe that unseen and seen forces create the influence, grace, and NEW NOTORIETY we seek.

We believe that success requires both heart and love.

We believe that success doesn't look the same to two people.

We believe that our role as leaders is to influence intelligently the people we are called to serve.

We believe that our personalities, ability, and authentic reactions are greater than our habits.

We believe that there is a solution to everything.

We believe that in stepping out into our true calling we make it easier for the ones around us to step out in theirs.

We believe that we must take care of ourselves before we can serve others.

We believe that we must rebel against social programming, pull down the hologram of pain, and step into our heart's desire to truly have the life of NEW NOTORIETY.

ABOUT THE AUTHOR

Three-time best-selling author and luxury NEURO HUMAN BRANDING expert, Ali Craig, combines over twenty years of real world, how to, goal achieving success into one book.

Ali Craig shares the real stories, science, and spirituality of how people have broken through the mediocrity of social success to discover their Success Rebel way. By allowing them to live their dreams and eventually living a life of influence, grace, and NEW NOTORIETY. In her latest work, Craig breaks through the social stories and subconscious triggers that she has helped so many of her entrepreneurial client struggle with over the years as they strive for success on their terms.

A sought-after national media expert in the United States and international speaker, Ali Craig, is the creator of the widely respected NERI profiling method and is the founder of the International Society of Intelligent Influence. Craig also is the founder of Entreventure Productions, Entreventure Events, and the Notoriety Network projects all designed to empower the modern-day entrepreneur.

Ali Craig splits her time between New York City, Las Vegas, Nevada, and Phoenix, Arizona where she is a kitty mom to eight wildly spoiled cats.

Sister Brands.

Hey Beautiful,

Yes, within these pages I talked about a lot of businesses and many of them are mine. Every single company - besides being separate legal entities and governed under their own unique rules and disclaimers (read that as check out each website for all of the legal specifics) - were created out of my SOULFIRE.

For me my SOULFIRE is all about creating and protecting beauty and love on this side of Heaven.

> What is more beautiful, and honoring, than helping a fellow human birth their SOULFIRE and DIVINE PARTNERSHIP into life?

> Helping another human feel connected, understand themselves better, or create relationships that are deep and meaningful in a timely manner.

> Or discovering that everything that they have been told that is wrong inside of them is perfect, beautiful, and is the exact Divine message needed to transform their lives and the lives of the ones they influence.

Yes, my SOULFIRE has shown up in many variations over the years. But the heart of my heart has always been the same - to create and protect beauty and love.

Today I have a few projects that help me create and protect beauty and love for myself, fellow entrepreneurs, the people we serve, and the world at large through our Success Rebel Society, Success Rebel Academy, NERI, Society of NEURO HUMAN BRANDING and the International Society of Intelligent Influence. I invite you to explore and see what my DIVINE PARTNERSHIP has created.

My intention for every engagement with you is that you know that you are loved, know that you are not alone, and are reminded of the Divine that lives inside of you. You can check out all of my sister brands at:

http://alicraig.com/sisterbrands

ACKNOWLEDGEMENTS

This book was a decade in the making because it took me that long to overcome the social stories of The OTHERS to not only write it, but to live it.

Thank you to the team of people who never stopped believing in me even though I kept moving this project off in the line of the sand of soon.

Thank you to everyone who held the space and my schedule so when I chose to make this a line in the concrete project, it was done.

Thank you for the DIVINE PARTNERSHIP who truly did write this book. Allowing me to merely be the hands, feet, and face of a project that is so much bigger than me.

DEDICATION

This book is dedicated to....

My Mom, Dad, and Sister who have taught me more on this side of Heaven than they could ever know. I am so glad my soul chose you. I love you.

The Black Sheep, Rebels, and Rule Breakers - remember, you feel more because you are meant for more. So, keep up the good fight. You got this. And I love you.

All the people who were and are pawns in the games of The OTHERS:

> I forgive you for your actions.
>
> I love you for your soul.
>
> Your intent was/ is terminated, and I have / am transformed.
>
> Thank you for the lessons. Now I am living my legacy.
>
> I love you.

354

www.ingramcontent.com/pod-product-compliance
Lightning Source LLC
Chambersburg PA
CBHW050233270326
41914CB00033BB/1895/J